JUNIOR GREAT BOOKS

SERIES 5

BOOK ONE

◆   ◆   ◆

The interpretive discussion program that moves

students toward excellence in reading comprehension,

critical thinking, and writing

JUNIOR GREAT BOOKS®

SERIES 5   BOOK ONE

THE GREAT BOOKS FOUNDATION
A nonprofit educational organization

Copyright © 2006 by The Great Books Foundation

Chicago, Illinois

All rights reserved

ISBN 978-1-933147-06-2

9   8   7   6

Printed in the United States of America

Published and distributed by

THE GREAT BOOKS FOUNDATION
A nonprofit educational organization

35 East Wacker Drive, Suite 400

Chicago, IL 60601

CONTENTS

THE NO-GUITAR BLUES

Gary Soto

The moment Fausto saw the group Los Lobos on *American Bandstand,* he knew exactly what he wanted to do with his life—play guitar. His eyes grew large with excitement as Los Lobos ground out a song while teenagers bounced off each other on the crowded dance floor.

He had watched *American Bandstand* for years and had heard Ray Camacho and the Teardrops at Romain Playground, but it had never occurred to him that he too might become a musician. That afternoon Fausto knew his mission in life: to play guitar in his own band, to sweat out his songs and prance around the stage, to make money and dress weird.

Fausto turned off the television set and walked outside, wondering how he could get enough money to buy a guitar. He couldn't ask his parents because they would just say, "Money doesn't grow on trees" or "What do you think we are, bankers?" And besides, they hated rock music. They were into the *conjunto* music of Lydia Mendoza, Flaco Jimenez, and Little Joe and La Familia. And, as Fausto recalled, the last album they bought was *The Chipmunks Sing Christmas Favorites*.

But what the heck, he'd give it a try. He returned inside and watched his mother make tortillas. He leaned against the kitchen counter, trying to work up the nerve to ask her for a guitar. Finally, he couldn't hold back any longer.

"Mom," he said, "I want a guitar for Christmas."

She looked up from rolling tortillas. "Honey, a guitar costs a lot of money."

"How 'bout for my birthday next year," he tried again.

"I can't promise," she said, turning back to her tortillas, "but we'll see."

Fausto walked back outside with a buttered tortilla. He knew his mother was right. His father was a warehouseman at Berven Rugs, where he made good money but not enough to buy everything his children wanted. Fausto decided to mow lawns to earn money, and was pushing the mower down the street before he realized it was winter and no one would hire him. He returned the mower and picked up a rake. He hopped onto his sister's bike (his had two flat tires) and rode north to the nicer section of Fresno in search of work. He went door-to-door, but after three hours he managed to get only one job, and not to rake leaves. He was asked to hurry down to the store to buy a loaf of bread, for which he received a grimy, dirt-caked quarter.

He also got an orange, which he ate sitting at the curb. While he was eating, a dog walked up and sniffed his leg. Fausto pushed him away and threw an orange peel skyward. The dog caught it and ate it in one gulp. The dog looked at Fausto and wagged his tail for more. Fausto tossed him a slice of orange, and the dog snapped it up and licked his lips.

"How come you like oranges, dog?"

The dog blinked a pair of sad eyes and whined.

"What's the matter? Cat got your tongue?" Fausto laughed at his joke and offered the dog another slice.

At that moment a dim light came on inside Fausto's head. He saw that it was sort of a fancy dog, a terrier or something, with dog tags and a shiny collar. And it looked well fed and healthy. In his neighborhood, the dogs were never licensed, and if they got sick they were placed near the water heater until they got well.

This dog looked like he belonged to rich people. Fausto cleaned his juice-sticky hands on his pants and got to his feet. The light in his head grew brighter. It just might work. He called the dog, patted its muscular back, and bent down to check the license.

"Great," he said. "There's an address."

The dog's name was Roger, which struck Fausto as weird because he'd never heard of a dog with a human name. Dogs should have names like Bomber, Freckles, Queenie, Killer, and Zero.

Fausto planned to take the dog home and collect a reward. He would say he had found Roger near the freeway. That would scare the daylights out of the owners, who would be so happy that they would probably give him a reward. He felt bad about lying, but the dog *was* loose. And it might even really be lost, because the address was six blocks away.

Fausto stashed the rake and his sister's bike behind a bush, and, tossing an orange peel every time Roger became distracted, walked the dog to his house. He hesitated on the porch until Roger began to scratch the door with a muddy paw. Fausto had come this far, so he figured he might as well go through with it. He knocked softly. When no one answered, he rang the doorbell. A man in a silky bathrobe and slippers opened the door and seemed confused by the sight of his dog and the boy.

"Sir," Fausto said, gripping Roger by the collar, "I found your dog by the freeway. His dog license says he lives here." Fausto looked down at the dog, then up to the man. "He does, doesn't he?"

The man stared at Fausto a long time before saying in a pleasant voice, "That's right." He pulled his robe tighter around him because of the cold and asked Fausto to come in. "So he was by the freeway?"

"Uh-huh."

"You bad, snoopy dog," said the man, wagging his finger. "You probably knocked over some trash cans, too, didn't you?"

Fausto didn't say anything. He looked around, amazed by this house with its shiny furniture and a television as large as the front window at home. Warm bread smells filled the air, and music full of soft tinkling floated in from another room.

"Helen," the man called to the kitchen, "we have a visitor." His wife came into the living room wiping her hands on a dish towel and smiling. "And who have we here?" she asked in one of the softest voices Fausto had ever heard.

"This young man said he found Roger near the freeway."

Fausto repeated his story to her while staring at a perpetual clock with a bell-shaped glass, the kind his aunt got when she celebrated her twenty-fifth anniversary. The lady frowned and said, wagging a finger at Roger, "Oh, you're a bad boy."

"It was very nice of you to bring Roger home," the man said. "Where do you live?"

"By that vacant lot on Olive," he said. "You know, by Brownie's Flower Place."

The wife looked at her husband, then Fausto. Her eyes twinkled triangles of light as she said, "Well, young man, you're probably hungry. How about a turnover?"

"What do I have to turn over?" Fausto asked, thinking she was talking about yard work or something like turning trays of dried raisins.

"No, no, dear, it's a pastry." She took him by the elbow and guided him to a kitchen that sparkled with copper pans and bright yellow wallpaper. She guided him to the kitchen table and gave him a tall glass of milk and something that looked like an *empanada*. Steamy waves of heat escaped when he tore it in two. He ate with both eyes on the man and woman who stood arm in arm smiling at him. They were strange, he thought. But nice.

"That was good," he said after he finished the turnover. "Did you make it, ma'am?"

"Yes, I did. Would you like another?"

"No, thank you. I have to go home now."

As Fausto walked to the door, the man opened his wallet and took out a bill. "This is for you," he said. "Roger is special to us, almost like a son."

Fausto looked at the bill and knew he was in trouble. Not with these nice folks or with his parents but with himself. How could he have been so deceitful? The dog wasn't lost. It was just having a fun Saturday walking around.

"I can't take that."

"You have to. You deserve it, believe me," the man said.

"No, I don't."

"Now don't be silly," said the lady. She took the bill from her husband and stuffed it into Fausto's shirt pocket. "You're a lovely child. Your parents are lucky to have you. Be good. And come see us again, please."

Fausto went out, and the lady closed the door. Fausto clutched the bill through his shirt pocket. He felt like ringing the doorbell and begging them to please take the money back, but he knew they would refuse. He hurried away, and at the end of the block, pulled the bill from his shirt pocket: it was a crisp twenty-dollar bill.

"Oh, man, I shouldn't have lied," he said under his breath as he started up the street like a zombie. He wanted to run to church for Saturday confession, but it was past four thirty, when confession stopped.

He returned to the bush where he had hidden the rake and his sister's bike and rode home slowly, not daring to touch the money in his pocket. At home, in the privacy of his room, he examined the twenty-dollar bill. He had never had so much money. It was probably enough to buy a secondhand guitar. But he felt bad, like the time he stole a dollar from the secret fold inside his older brother's wallet.

Fausto went outside and sat on the fence. "Yeah," he said. "I can probably get a guitar for twenty. Maybe at a yard sale—things are cheaper."

His mother called him to dinner.

The next day he dressed for church without anyone telling him. He was going to go to eight o'clock mass.

"I'm going to church, Mom," he said. His mother was in the kitchen cooking *papas* and *chorizo con huevos*. A pile of tortillas lay warm under a dishtowel.

"Oh, I'm so proud of you, son." She beamed, turning over the crackling *papas*.

His older brother, Lawrence, who was at the table reading the funnies, mimicked, "Oh, I'm so proud of you, my son," under his breath.

At Saint Theresa's he sat near the front. When Father Jerry began by saying that we are all sinners, Fausto thought he looked right at him. Could he know? Fausto

13

fidgeted with guilt. No, he thought. I only did it yesterday.

Fausto knelt, prayed, and sang. But he couldn't forget the man and the lady, whose names he didn't even know, and the *empanada* they had given him. It had a strange name but tasted really good. He wondered how they got rich. And how that dome clock worked. He had asked his mother once how his aunt's clock worked. She said it just worked, the way the refrigerator works. It just did.

Fausto caught his mind wandering and tried to concentrate on his sins. He said a Hail Mary and sang, and when the wicker basket came his way, he stuck a hand reluctantly in his pocket and pulled out the twenty-dollar bill. He ironed it between his palms, and dropped it into the basket. The grownups stared. Here was a kid dropping twenty dollars in the basket while they gave just three or four dollars.

There would be a second collection for Saint Vincent de Paul, the lector announced. The wicker baskets again floated in the pews, and this time the adults around him, given a second chance to show their charity, dug deep into their wallets and purses and dropped in fives and tens. This time Fausto tossed in the grimy quarter.

Fausto felt better after church. He went home and played football in the front yard with his brother and some neighbor kids. He felt cleared of wrongdoing and was so happy that he played one of his best games of football ever. On one play, he tore his good pants, which he knew he shouldn't have been wearing. For a second, while he examined the hole, he wished he hadn't given the twenty dollars away.

Man, I coulda bought me some Levi's, he thought. He pictured his twenty dollars being spent to buy church candles. He pictured a priest buying an armful of flowers with *his* money.

Fausto had to forget about getting a guitar. He spent the next day playing soccer in his good pants, which were now his old pants. But that night during dinner, his mother said she remembered seeing an old bass *guitarron* the last time she cleaned out her father's garage.

"It's a little dusty," his mom said, serving his favorite enchiladas, "but I think it works. Grandpa says it works."

Fausto's ears perked up. That was the same kind the guy in Los Lobos played. Instead of asking for the guitar, he waited for his mother to offer it to him. And she did, while gathering the dishes from the table.

"No, Mom, I'll do it," he said, hugging her. "I'll do the dishes forever if you want."

It was the happiest day of his life. No, it was the second-happiest day of his life. The happiest was when his grandfather Lupe placed the *guitarron*, which was nearly as huge as a washtub, in his arms. Fausto ran a thumb down the strings, which vibrated in his throat and chest. It sounded beautiful, deep and eerie. A pumpkin smile widened on his face.

"OK, *hijo*, now you put your fingers like this," said his grandfather, smelling of tobacco and aftershave. He took Fausto's fingers and placed them on the strings. Fausto strummed a chord on the *guitarron*, and the bass resounded in their chests.

The *guitarron* was more complicated than Fausto imagined. But he was confident that after a few more lessons he could start a band that would someday play on *American Bandstand* for the dancing crowds.

KADDO'S WALL

West African folktale as told by
Harold Courlander and George Herzog

In the town of Tendella in the Kingdom of Seno, north of the Gulf of Guinea, there was a rich man by the name of Kaddo. His fields spread out on every side of the town. At plowing time hundreds of men and boys hoed up his fields, and then hundreds of women and girls planted his corn seed in the ground for him. His grain bulged in his granary, because each season he harvested far more than he could use. The name of Kaddo was known far and wide throughout the Kingdom of Seno. Travelers who passed through the town carried tales of his wealth far beyond Seno's borders.

One day Kaddo called all of his people in the town of Tendella together for a big meeting in front of his house. They all came, for Kaddo was an important man, and they knew he was going to make an important announcement.

17

"There's something that bothers me," Kaddo said. "I've been thinking about it for a long time. I've lain awake worrying. I have so much corn in my granary that I don't know what to do with it."

The people listened attentively, and thought about Kaddo's words. Then a man said:

"Some of the people of the town have no corn at all. They are very poor and have nothing. Why don't you give some of your corn to them?"

Kaddo shook his head and said, "No, that isn't a very good idea. It doesn't satisfy me."

Another man said to Kaddo:

"Well, then, you could lend corn to the people who have had a bad harvest and have no seed for the spring planting. That would be very good for the town and would keep poverty away."

"No," Kaddo said, "that's no solution either."

"Well, then, why not sell some of your corn and buy cattle instead?" still another man said.

Kaddo shook his head.

"No, it's not very good advice. It's hard for people to advise a rich man with problems like mine."

Many people made suggestions, but nobody's advice suited Kaddo. He thought for a while, and at last he said:

"Send me as many young girls as you can find. I will have them grind the corn for me."

The people went away. They were angry with Kaddo. But the next day they sent a hundred girls to work for him as he had asked. On a hundred grindstones they began to grind Kaddo's corn into flour. All day long they put corn into the grindstones and took flour out. All day long the people of the town heard the sound of the grinding at Kaddo's house. A pile of corn flour began to grow. For seven days and seven nights the girls ground corn without a pause.

When the last grain of corn was ground into flour, Kaddo called the girls together and said:

"Now bring water from the spring. We shall mix it with the corn flour to make mortar out of it."

So the girls brought water in water pots and mixed it with the flour to make a thick mortar. Then Kaddo ordered them to make bricks out of the mortar.

"When the bricks are dry, then I shall make a wall of them around my house," he said.

Word went out that Kaddo was preparing to build a wall of flour around his house, and the people of the town came to his door and protested.

"You can't do a thing like this, it is against humanity!" they said.

"It's not right, people have no right to build walls with food!" a man said.

"Ah, what is right and what is wrong?" Kaddo said. "My right is different from yours, because I am so very rich. So leave me alone."

"Corn is to eat, so that you may keep alive," another said. "It's not meant to taunt those who are less fortunate."

19

"When people are hungry it is an affront to shut them out with a wall of flour," another man said.

"Stop your complaints," Kaddo said. "The corn is mine. It is my surplus. I can't eat it all. It comes from my own fields. I am rich. What good is it to be rich if you can't do what you want with your own property?"

The people of the town went away, shaking their heads in anger over Kaddo's madness. The hundred girls continued to make bricks of flour, which they dried in the sun. And when the bricks were dry Kaddo had them begin building the wall around his house. They used wet dough for mortar to hold the bricks together, and slowly the wall grew. They stuck cowry shells into the wall to make beautiful designs, and when at last the wall was done, and the last corn flour used up, Kaddo was very proud. He walked back and forth and looked at his wall. He walked around it. He went in and out of the gate. He was very happy.

And now when people came to see him they had to stand by the gate until he asked them to enter. When the workers who plowed and planted for Kaddo wanted to talk to him, Kaddo sat on the wall by the gate and listened to them and gave them orders. And whenever the people of the town wanted his opinion on an important matter he sat on his wall and gave it to them, while they stood and listened.

Things went on like this for a long time. Kaddo enjoyed his reputation as the richest man for miles

around. The story of Kaddo's wall went to the farthest
parts of the kingdom.

And then one year there was a bad harvest for Kaddo.
There wasn't enough rain to grow the corn, and the earth
dried up hard and dusty like the road. There wasn't a
single ear of corn in all of Kaddo's fields or the fields of
his relatives.

The next year it was the same. Kaddo had no seed
corn left, so he sold his cattle and horses to buy corn for
food and seed for a new planting. He sowed corn again,
but the next harvest time it was the same, and there
wasn't a single ear of corn on all his fields.

Year after year Kaddo's crops failed. Some of his
relatives died of hunger, and others went away to other
parts of the Kingdom of Seno, for they had no more seed
corn to plant and they couldn't count on Kaddo's help.
Kaddo's workers ran away, because he was unable to feed
them. Gradually Kaddo's part of the town became
deserted. All that he had left were a young daughter and
a mangy donkey.

When his cattle and his money were all gone, Kaddo
became very hungry. He scraped away a little bit of the
flour wall and ate it. The next day he scraped away more
of the flour wall and ate it. The wall got lower and lower.
Little by little it disappeared. A day came when the wall
was gone, when nothing was left of the elegant structure
Kaddo had built around his house, and on which he had
used to sit to listen to the people of the town when they
came to ask him to lend them a little seed corn.

Then Kaddo realized that if he was to live any longer he must get help from somewhere. He wondered who would help him. Not the people of Tendella, for he had insulted and mistreated them and they would have nothing to do with him. There was only one man he could go to, Sogole, king of the Ganna people, who had the reputation of being very rich and generous.

So Kaddo and his daughter got on the mangy, underfed donkey and rode seven days until they arrived in the land of the Ganna.

Sogole sat before his royal house when Kaddo arrived. He had a soft skin put on the ground next to him for Kaddo to sit upon, and had millet beer brought for the two of them to drink.

"Well, stranger in the land of the Ganna, take a long drink, for you have a long trip behind you if you come from Tendella," Sogole said.

"Thank you, but I can't drink much," Kaddo said.

"Why is that?" Sogole said. "When people are thirsty they drink."

"That is true," Kaddo replied. "But I have been hungry too long, and my stomach is shrunk."

"Well, drink in peace then, because now that you are my guest you won't be hungry. You shall have whatever you need from me."

Kaddo nodded his head solemnly and drank a little of the millet beer.

"And now tell me," Sogole said. "You say you come from the town of Tendella in the Kingdom of Seno?

I've heard many tales of that town. The famine came there and drove out many people, because they had no corn left."

"Yes," Kaddo said. "Hard times drove them out, and the corn was all gone."

"But tell me, there was a rich and powerful man in Tendella named Kaddo, wasn't there? What ever happened to him? Is he still alive?"

"Yes, he is still alive," Kaddo said.

"A fabulous man, this Kaddo," Sogole said. "They say he built a wall of flour around his house out of his surplus crops, and when he talked to his people he sat on the wall by his gate. Is this true?"

"Yes, it is true," Kaddo said sadly.

"Does he still have as many cattle as he used to?" Sogole asked.

"No, they are all gone."

"It is an unhappy thing for a man who owned so much to come to so little," Sogole said. "But doesn't he have many servants and workers still?"

"His workers and servants are all gone," Kaddo said. "Of all his great household he has only one daughter left. The rest went away because there was no money and no food."

Sogole looked melancholy.

"Ah, what is a rich man when his cattle are gone and his servants have left him? But tell me, what happened to the wall of flour that he built around his house?"

"He ate the wall," Kaddo said. "Each day he scraped a little of the flour from the wall, until it was all gone."

"A strange story," Sogole said. "But such is life."

And he thought quietly for a while about the way life goes for people sometimes, and then he asked:

"And were you, by any chance, one of Kaddo's family?"

"Indeed I was one of Kaddo's family. Once I was rich. Once I had more cattle than I could count. Once I had many cornfields. Once I had hundreds of workers cultivating my crops. Once I had a bursting granary. Once I was Kaddo, the great personage of Tendella."

"What! You yourself are Kaddo?"

"Yes, once I was proud and lordly, and now I sit in rags begging for help."

"What can I do for you?" Sogole asked.

"I have nothing left now. Give me some seed corn, so that I can go back and plant my fields again."

"Take what you need," Sogole said. He ordered his servants to bring bags of corn and to load them on Kaddo's donkey. Kaddo thanked him humbly, and he and his daughter started their return trip to Tendella. They traveled for seven days. On the way Kaddo became very hungry. He hadn't seen so much corn for a long time as he was bringing back from the Kingdom of the Ganna. He took a few grains and put them in his mouth and chewed them. Once more he put a few grains in his mouth. Then he put a whole handful in his mouth and swallowed. He couldn't stop. He ate and ate. He forgot that this was the corn with which he had to plant his fields. When he arrived in Tendella he went to his bed to sleep, and when he arose the next morning he ate again. He ate so much of the corn that he became sick. He went to his bed again and cried out in pain, because his stomach had forgotten what to do with food. And before long Kaddo died.

Kaddo's grandchildren and great-grandchildren in the Kingdom of Seno are poor to this day. And to the rich men of the country the common people sometimes say:

"Don't build a wall of flour around your house."

TURQUOISE HORSE

Gerald Hausman

Some years ago, in Navajo country, there was a girl named Lisa Todachine whose father was a silversmith.

When Lisa was twelve years old, she had a dream in which she chased a horse. She was on foot in the dream, and the horse raced ahead of her, dancing on small delicate hooves.

The dream came again and again. During the day Lisa did not think about the dream, nor did she mention it to anyone. But at night, before she went to sleep, she remembered the horse, and it made her sad to think that though she saw the horse every night, her dream was always in black and white.

There came a night when the dream changed into color. Lisa was running along a narrow trail upon a vast mesa and the horse was ahead of her, its mane flashing in the wind, its forehooves striking sparks on the hard-packed earth.

When it happened she was not surprised but pleased. The horse reared magnificently on a rock outcropping, and then, in a blaze of blue it transformed into a turquoise horse. The moment this happened Lisa knew she was in a dream, because in real life there is no such thing as blue horses. And then the horse did a wonderful thing. Rearing over the verge, it suddenly leaped into the open, empty air and, pawing miraculously, found its footing in the sky. Then it whinnied triumphantly and galloped off across the clouds.

The next morning Lisa went to where her father worked on his jewelry behind their hogan. In the warm seasons, summer and fall, he usually did his work under a four-post juniper shelter, the upper latillas of which were spindly bark-peeled branches. Shadows fell in clean lines at his feet. He worked in the cool of this outdoor workshop until, little by little, the sun grew bolder and bolder and stole all the way into the shadow of the shelter.

Lisa liked to watch her father work. His composure seemed cast of the same fire-blackened silver as his bracelets, rings, and pins. He was a man of mud and fire, blood and bone whose surface was etched and hammered by years of sun and rain. He knew what it meant to make a mold and what it meant, as a grown man, to have been molded by nature.

Lisa knew that her father was wise. She also knew that he was certain of the old ways that had been taught to him by his own father. From father to son, mother to

27

daughter the teachings came down, year after year, sun after moon.

"Father," Lisa said, "I have a dream to tell you."

She waited while he removed a casting from the hot coals before which, holding iron tongs in a pair of heavy cowhide gloves, he sat back on the heels of his elk moccasins.

"Yes," he said, finally. "Tell me your dream."

"There is a horse. I run after it, but I can never catch it. Mostly the horse is dark because I dream this dream in black and white. But last night, for the first time, the horse looked me in the eyes. I heard it snort loudly before it turned turquoise and galloped away into the clouds. Father, I need to know what this dream means, for I have it every night."

Lisa's father said nothing, nor did he look into his daughter's worried face. He bent over his tufa-casting and tapped it with a little hammer.

Lisa knew that her father was not ignoring her. He was not, as it appeared, concentrating only on his work. He was, she knew, thinking deeply about what she had told him.

Then he got slowly to his feet and stretched his arms.

"You get stiff in that position," he said, then, "Come with me for a moment, Lisa."

Together, they walked on the dry wash just below where her father worked. A little ribbon of water, sky colored, shivered between the clay banks that rose above their shoulders.

After walking for a few minutes, her father stopped.

"I think it was here," he said. "Yes, I am certain of it, here."

"What?" Lisa asked.

"I was your age, maybe a little younger when I made the discovery. Do you see where the water runs down from high up on the hill? Where there is now a dry scar on that cliff?"

Lisa nodded. In rainy times, such soft eroded places sang full throated with tumbling water. If you were not careful, when the water ran at its fullest, you could be swept to your death.

"When I was your age," Lisa's father began, "I was caught in one of those sudden storms. The whole hillside seemed to come down on my head. I got swept away. A big juniper branch saved my life. I held on to it for all I was worth. When my grandfather pulled me to safety, we both stopped in our tracks. For directly in front of us was a ruined grave, one that the wild waters had ripped apart. There was silver everywhere, for as you know, the dear possessions of the dead are buried with the body."

Lisa's father turned on his moccasined heel and began to walk back to his workshop on the hill above the arroyo.

"What does this mean, Father?" she asked.

"In all that silver, there was a bracelet, that even now after all the years, I remember as if it were yesterday. The silversmith had made that bracelet a hundred years ago, and yet it was as new as the day he measured the wrist that wore it . . . a wrist that was once flesh and bone, a wrist that is now dust."

"What did you do with the bracelet?"

Looking at his daughter for the first time, Lisa's father smiled a little crookedly. She knew what that meant. Trouble. A lesson. She had said something wrong.

"You know it is a bad thing to disturb the sacred places of burial. I did nothing with the bracelet. I merely looked at it. I took it with my eyes, for a moment, and held it there. Then my grandfather and I walked on and we erased that place from our memory. It is only now, as you told me of your dream, that I remembered."

"That gravesite," Lisa said, "was ruined in the rain. You didn't know where the real location of the grave was, only where the jewelry turned up at your feet."

"That is right."

"Then why couldn't you take it and give it a proper home? Otherwise it could've been taken by someone less than yourself, a thief perhaps."

"To take that which does not belong to you, no matter the circumstances, is a bad thing. Let the runner run, the walker walk, and the thief thieve. You can't change that which is—the rain, the runoff, the broken grave. We didn't touch that silverwork. Perhaps it's still there, perhaps not. It doesn't matter. What is important is that we saw the bracelet with our eyes . . . we embraced it. From that moment on, I knew I would be a silversmith."

"But how did you know?"

"I knew because I understood—having almost drowned—that only those things which live are worth living for."

Lisa said, "I understand now."

"There is something else," her father said kneeling before his dwindling fire. "The thing that made the bracelet so beautiful was the turquoise horse that decorated it. I've never forgotten that horse that seemed to be dancing on a cloud."

Lisa waited for him to say something more, but he busied himself with his casting.

That night Lisa dreamed the dream of the turquoise horse, and again, she saw it in color. This time the horse danced upon a cloud, just as her father had said, and it beckoned her to follow. She was afraid. Backing away from the edge of the great cliff where the horse had taken its swift leap into the air, she felt fear in her throat.

"I can't come with you," she said to the horse, "I can't walk on air."

Then the horse galloped to the mesa, and kneeling as her father had knelt before the fire, it bowed its head. Lisa had only to take one step and she would be on its back. She hesitated, and then heard the voice that came from the clouds.

The voice said, "The turquoise horse is yours now."

It was a command and Lisa obeyed.

The horse got to its feet and in one graceful bound, tossing its neck to the east, it dropped off the cliff like falling water. Then it flailed its hooves on the air, parted the clouds, swam up into the sky.

Lisa clung to the horse's mane, but she did not feel fearful. Easily, dreamily, like flowing silk, she let the horse have its head. And the horse plunged higher into the cliffs of cloud and was swallowed up.

Then she felt her body melt as the vapors wrapped her round, and the voice of the cloud-person spoke again.

Lisa could see nothing, for the mist was everywhere. She felt the gleaming flank muscle of the turquoise horse. This was real, she told herself, the voice of the cloud-person was real.

Then the world, the universe stood still, the clouds froze and everything turned into still-life.

"Hear me," the cloud-person said, "I am of the family of the Sun. The horse you ride on belongs to us. But we do not own him. No one can own the Turquoise Horse."

Lisa woke with a start. It was morning, the weekend was over and it was time to get dressed for school. The dream she'd been having dissolved in her waking mind. She got dressed, put her books in her bookbag, and had breakfast with her mother and father. They ate in silence. Morning was quiet time. It was not necessary to speak. Instead they listened.

At school Lisa remained quiet. In little bits throughout the morning her dream returned, giving her no peace. It was only after lunch, after she had gone running several miles with her friends, that she realized how tired she was, how her dream had physically drained her.

Back in the classroom, her teacher introduced a folksinger, a man with a handlebar mustache who had been assigned to their school district by the Arizona Commission on the Arts. He walked about the room, plunking a banjo and urging the children to write verses of a song that all of them would compose together.

She liked the tune and the verses rolled out, tinkly and funny, and they made her forget her dream. All the students in the room were laughing and the mustached man made his banjo ring: "Put your head on the floor, pick it up, pick it up; put your head on the floor, pick it up, pick it up."

Lisa could not help smiling at this man who was all smiles himself. Although he was not Navajo, there was something Indian about him. He didn't act like a white person. Like her father, he was sure of something. That something was inside the tight white drum head of his banjo.

If only she were sure . . . if only she had something she were certain of . . . the banjo rang for the last time. Then it was time for the students to write their own composition, something of their own, which the mustache-man would put to music for the following day.

Lisa wasn't going to write anything. She doodled on the creamy sheet of paper that covered her desktop. But her doodling, mindless and abstract, changed into something else. She began to draw the turquoise horse. The moment she saw its image drawn by her own hand on paper, she heard the words of the cloud-person.

I am the Sun's son.
I sit upon a turquoise horse
   at the opening
   of the sky.

My horse walks
   on the upper circle
   of the rainbow.

My horse has a sunbeam
for a bridle.

My horse circles
   all the people
   of the earth.

Today, I, Lisa Todachine, ride
upon his broad back
and he is mine.

Tomorrow
he will belong to another.

The drawing and the words came out of her so fast, she didn't have time to think about them. Then they were collected by the folksinger whose name was John Arrowsmith. For a moment, when he came to each desk to pick up the papers, she felt him touch her and his hand was rough as sandpaper, not soft the way she imagined a musician's hand should feel, but hard like her father's.

That night Lisa did not dream. Restlessly, she tossed and turned in her sleep. When morning came, she was unwell. Her father, already out in his workshop by the time she started breakfast, was striking silver with his hammer, and the ting-tang of his hammer made her think of the folksinger named John Arrowsmith. Prickles when she thought of him. Her poem. She was afraid . . . but was it a poem? . . . she did not know.

After breakfast, on her way to the bus stop, Lisa visited her father. He was in that meditative morning mood. Not a good time to disturb him, but she had to.

"Father, I've done a bad thing," she said.

Quickly her father's eyes met her own. Then he looked away, waiting politely for her to speak. He didn't busy himself with his jewelry this time. His hands were folded in his lap, and he waited.

"I dreamed of the turquoise horse," she said gently. "No, I dreamed not of him, I dreamed I was part of him, that I rode him all the way to the top of the sky. There I met a cloud-person who told me that the horse belonged to him. I was permitted to ride the turquoise horse, but it belonged to the family of the sun."

"You've dreamed a great dream, Lisa. You rode the turquoise horse; you've been embraced by the holy people."

He looked awed by this and she burst into tears.

He reached toward her without actually touching her, his hands outstretched, his palms open, asking.

"You don't understand," she sobbed. "Yesterday, a musician came to our class, and I liked his music. I liked him. I liked the way he played his banjo, it made everyone happy.

"This is foolish, I know. That is why I am crying. And because I think I've done a bad thing. The singer asked us to write a poem which he would put to music. I wrote about the turquoise horse. Today, I think he will sing about it, and I am ashamed. This is like taking the silver bracelet from the spoiled grave. I had no right to tell my dream in words and put them on paper. I have stolen from a sacred grave. I am a thief."

As she said these words, her father listened without expression. When she was done, he broke into a smile.

"You have not stolen anything, child. You were given something. A blessed thing that dream was . . . but how you choose to share it is up to you—your decision, and yours alone. Remember, in the dream, the cloud-person said the horse was for all to share."

"But what if he takes my song and sells it and makes money from it. It would be a sin."

Sighing, her father said, "The world's made up of many people. Not all are righteous—but the cloud-person trusted you . . . now you must trust yourself."

That day passed slowly for Lisa. She could hear what people said to her, but they seemed to speak from such a distance, and their voices were almost inaudible. Even on the playground, shouts of her friends came to her in muffled silence. She was waiting, waiting for the moment when he would walk into the room and sing her song. She could hear his banjo ringing, his happy mustached face glowing as he sang her song. But at the same time, regardless of what her father said, she felt the awful shame of the betrayed secret. She wanted to bury her song, to hide it away forever.

At last the moment she'd been anticipating arrived. John Arrowsmith came into the classroom. He took out his banjo and tuned it. Then he spread four pieces of art paper on a desk.

"These are your songs," he said, "and I'm going to sing them for you. Naturally, I wish I had the time to make tunes for all the things you wrote, but I only had one night . . . anyway, here goes . . ."

John Arrowsmith sang four songs, one right after the other. The class loved them. One about a goat that butted everyone; one about a house that flew up to the moon; one with a catchy tune that went—"People these days should be nice to each other, people these days have to care for one another, people these days, people these days . . ."

Lisa didn't hear her song though. He probably hadn't even read it. The hollow feeling inside her got bigger. She was relieved because the secret of the turquoise horse was still a secret. And yet, she was disappointed. . . .

After school, walking toward the bus, she saw John Arrowsmith about to get into his pickup truck. He gave her a big smile and a wave.

"You're Lisa, aren't you?"

She stopped in her tracks as he came over, his leather briefcase in hand. He had on a black cowboy hat with a horsehair hatband. Close up, he was rougher looking than she thought. Like his hands, he was weathered in the face.

"Did I get your name right?" he asked gently.

"I'm Lisa Todachine."

"Doesn't that name mean bitterwater? If so your father's the silversmith. I'm wearing one of his buckles."

Lisa felt the warmth come around her. She liked him. She was right to have trusted him.

"He's a silversmith, while you are a poet! I didn't sing your song today because I felt it was private, something between you and your family maybe. Well, there's another reason, too. I don't think it's really a song. There may be a fine line of difference between a song and a poem, but I think this is a poem. When you decide to really share it with people, you might think about putting it in a book."

Lisa blushed.

"Well, so long." He handed the poem back to her.

"Poem," she said to herself. What a funny word. What a funny, lovely, feeling-kind-of-word.

When she got back to her home, she put the poem of the turquoise horse on the wall of her room where anyone could see it . . . anyone in her family, that is.

But she knew, because she had changed, that her family was growing. It now included her father and mother, her mother's family and her father's family, a cloud-person and a turquoise horse, a folksinger named John Arrowsmith, and people she had not even met who would one day read her poems in a book.

She was going to have a big family, of that she was sure.

A Game of Catch

Richard Wilbur

Monk and Glennie were playing catch on the side lawn of the firehouse when Scho caught sight of them. They were good at it, for seventh-graders, as anyone could see right away. Monk, wearing a catcher's mitt, would lean easily sidewise and back, with one leg lifted and his throwing hand almost down to the grass, and then lob the white ball straight up into the sunlight. Glennie would shield his eyes with his left hand and, just as the ball fell past him, snag it with a little dart of his glove. Then he would burn the ball straight toward Monk, and it would spank into the round mitt and sit, like a still-life apple on a plate, until Monk flipped it over into his right hand and, with a negligent flick of his hanging arm, gave Glennie a fast grounder.

They were going on and on like that, in a kind of slow, mannered, luxurious dance in the sun, their faces

39

perfectly blank and entranced, when Glennie noticed Scho dawdling along the other side of the street and called hello to him. Scho crossed over and stood at the front edge of the lawn, near an apple tree, watching.

"Got your glove?" asked Glennie after a time. Scho obviously hadn't.

"You could give me some easy grounders," said Scho. "But don't burn 'em."

"All right," Glennie said. He moved off a little, so the three of them formed a triangle, and they passed the ball around for about five minutes, Monk tossing easy grounders to Scho, Scho throwing to Glennie, and Glennie burning them in to Monk. After a while, Monk began to throw them back to Glennie once or twice before he let Scho have his grounder, and finally Monk gave Scho a fast, bumpy grounder that hopped over his shoulder and went into the brake on the other side of the street.

"Not so hard," called Scho as he ran across to get it.

"You should've had it," Monk shouted.

It took Scho a little while to find the ball among the ferns and dead leaves, and when he saw it, he grabbed it up and threw it toward Glennie. It struck the trunk of the apple tree, bounced back at an angle, and rolled steadily and stupidly onto the cement apron in front of the firehouse, where one of the trucks was parked. Scho ran hard and stopped it just before it rolled under the truck, and this time he carried it back to his former position on the lawn and threw it carefully to Glennie.

"I got an idea," said Glennie. "Why don't Monk and I catch for five minutes more, and then you can borrow one of our gloves?"

"That's all right with me," said Monk. He socked his fist into his mitt, and Glennie burned one in.

"All right," Scho said, and went over and sat under the tree. There in the shade he watched them resume their skillful play. They threw lazily fast or lazily slow—high, low, or wide—and always handsomely, their expressions serene, changeless, and forgetful. When Monk missed a low backhand catch, he walked indolently after the ball and, hardly even looking, flung it sidearm for an imaginary putout. After a good while of this, Scho said, "Isn't it five minutes yet?"

"One minute to go," said Monk, with a fraction of a grin.

Scho stood up and watched the ball slap back and forth for several minutes more, and then he turned and pulled himself up into the crotch of the tree.

"Where are you going?" Monk asked.

"Just up the tree," Scho said.

"I guess he doesn't want to catch," said Monk.

Scho went up and up through the fat, light gray branches until they grew slender and bright and gave under him. He found a place where several supple branches were knit to make a dangerous chair, and sat there with his head coming out of the leaves into the sunlight. He could see the two other boys down below, the ball going back and forth between them as if they

41

were bowling on the grass, and Glennie's crew-cut head looking like a sea urchin.

"I found a wonderful seat up here," Scho said loudly. "If I don't fall out." Monk and Glennie didn't look up or comment, and so he began jouncing gently in his chair of branches and singing "Yo-ho, heave ho" in an exaggerated way.

"Do you know what, Monk?" he announced in a few moments. "I can make you two guys do anything I want. Catch that ball, Monk! Now you catch it, Glennie!"

"I was going to catch it anyway," Monk suddenly said. "You're not making anybody do anything when they're already going to do it anyway."

"I made you say what you just said," Scho replied joyfully.

"No, you didn't," said Monk, still throwing and catching but now less serenely absorbed in the game.

"That's what I wanted you to say," Scho said.

The ball bounded off the rim of Monk's mitt and plowed into a gladiolus bed beside the firehouse, and Monk ran to get it while Scho jounced in his treetop and sang, "I wanted you to miss that. Anything you do is what I wanted you to do."

"Let's quit for a minute," Glennie suggested.

"We might as well, until the peanut gallery shuts up," Monk said.

They went over and sat cross-legged in the shade of the tree. Scho looked down between his legs and saw them on the dim, spotty ground, saying nothing to one another. Glennie soon began abstractedly spinning his glove between his palms; Monk pulled his nose and stared out across the lawn.

"I want you to mess around with your nose, Monk," said Scho, giggling. Monk withdrew his hand from his face.

"Do that with your glove, Glennie," Scho persisted. "Monk, I want you to pull up hunks of grass and chew on it."

Glennie looked up and saw a self-delighted, intense face staring down at him through the leaves. "Stop being a dope and come down and we'll catch for a few minutes," he said.

Scho hesitated, and then said, in a tentatively mocking voice, "That's what I wanted you to say."

"All right, then, nuts to you," said Glennie.

"Why don't you keep quiet and stop bothering people?" Monk asked.

"I made you say that," Scho replied, softly.

"Shut up," Monk said.

"I made you say that, and I want you to be standing there looking sore. And I want you to climb up the tree. I'm making you do it!"

Monk was scrambling up through the branches, awkward in his haste, and getting snagged on twigs. His face was furious and foolish, and he kept telling Scho to shut up, shut up, shut up, while the other's exuberant and panicky voice poured down upon his head.

"Now you shut up or you'll be sorry," Monk said, breathing hard as he reached up and threatened to shake the cradle of slight branches in which Scho was sitting.

"I *want*—" Scho screamed as he fell. Two lower branches broke his rustling, crackling fall, but he landed on his back with a deep thud and lay still, with a strangled look on his face and his eyes clenched. Glennie knelt down and asked breathlessly, "Are you OK, Scho? Are you OK?" while Monk swung down through the leaves crying that honestly he hadn't even touched him, the crazy guy just let go. Scho doubled up and turned over on his right side, and now both the other boys knelt beside him, pawing at his shoulder and begging to know how he was.

Then Scho rolled away from them and sat partly up, still struggling to get his wind but forcing a species of smile onto his face.

"I'm sorry, Scho," Monk said. "I didn't mean to make you fall."

Scho's voice came out weak and gravelly, in gasps. "I meant—you to do it. You—had to. You can't do—anything—unless I want—you to."

Glennie and Monk looked helplessly at him as he sat there, breathing a bit more easily and smiling fixedly, with tears in his eyes. Then they picked up their gloves and the ball, walked over to the street, and went slowly away down the sidewalk, Monk punching his fist into the mitt, Glennie juggling the ball between glove and hand.

From under the apple tree, Scho, still bent over a little for lack of breath, croaked after them in triumph and misery, "I want you to do whatever you're going to do for the whole rest of your life!"

Oliver Hyde's Dishcloth Concert

Richard Kennedy

Now maybe it's sad and maybe it's spooky, but there was a man who lived just out of town on a scrubby farm and no one had seen his face for years. If he was outside working, he kept his hat pulled down and his collar turned up, and if anyone approached him he ran up the hill to his house and shut himself inside. He left notes pinned to his door for a brave errand boy who brought him supplies from town. The people asked the boy what he heard up there in that tomblike house when he collected the notes and delivered the supplies. "Darkness and quietness," said the boy. "I hear darkness and quietness." The people nodded and looked at the boy. "Aren't you afraid?" The boy bit his lip. "A fellow has to make a living," he said.

Sometimes the children would come out of town and sing a little song up at the house and then run away. They sang:

The beautiful bride of Oliver Hyde,
Fell down dead on the mountainside.

Yes, it was true. The man was full of grief and bitterness. He was Oliver Hyde, and his young bride's wagon had been washed into a canyon by a mudslide and it killed her, horse and all. But that was years ago. The children sang some more:

Oliver Hyde is a strange old man,
He sticks his head in a coffee can,
And hides his face when there's folks about,
He's outside in, and he's inside out.

It was too bad. Oliver used to have many friends, and he played the fastest and sweetest fiddle in the county. And for the few short weeks he was married his playing was sweeter than ever. But on the day his wife was buried he busted his fiddle across a porch post, and now he sat cold, dark, and quiet on his little hill. No one had visited him for years. There was a reason. You shall see.

One day a man came from the town and walked up the hill toward Oliver's house. He was carrying a fiddle case. Two or three times he stopped and looked up at the house and shook his head, as if trying to free himself from a ghost, and continued on. He arrived at the porch steps. All the window shades were pulled down and it was dead quiet inside. The three porch steps creaked like cats moaning in their dreams, and the man knocked on the door. For a little bit it was quiet, then there was the sound of a chair being scooted across the floor. A voice said, "Come in."

The man opened the door a crack and peeked inside.

"Oliver?" he said. "It's me, Jim." No answer. Jim opened the door farther and put a foot inside. It was dark and smelled stale. Jim opened the door all the way.

Off in a corner where the light didn't touch sat a figure in a chair, perfectly upright, with his hands on his knees like a stone god, as still and silent as a thousand years ago. The head was draped completely with a dishcloth. Not a breath ruffled the ghost head.

Jim swallowed and spoke. "Haven't seen you around lately, Oliver." No answer.

People used to visit Oliver for a while after his beautiful bride fell down dead on the mountainside, but this is how it was—Oliver sitting in the dark with a dishcloth over his head, and he never spoke to them. It was too strange. His friends stopped visiting.

All Jim wanted was a single word from Oliver—yes or no. He had a favor to ask. He was Oliver's oldest friend. He moved inside.

"Sue's getting married, Oliver," he said. No answer. "You remember my little girl, Sue? She's all growed up now, Oliver, and mighty pretty, too." For all the notice he got, Jim might just as well have been talking to a stove. He cleared his voice and went on. "The reason I came, Oliver, was to ask you to come and play the fiddle for us at the dance. We was the best friends, and I don't see how I can marry off Sue without you being there to fiddle for us. You can just say yes or no, Oliver."

Now Oliver wasn't dead himself yet, so he still had feelings, and Jim had been his best friend. They had played and fought together, fished and hunted, and grown up together. So Oliver hated to say "No" just flat out like that, so he said instead, "No fiddle." Jim was prepared for that, and he laid the fiddle case down on the floor and flipped it open.

"Here, I brought a fiddle, Oliver. Porky Fellows was happy to make a lend of it."

Oliver felt trapped now. He was silent for a long time, then finally he said, "Tell you what. I can't wear this dishcloth on my head and fiddle, but if everyone else wears a dishcloth I'll come."

Jim was quiet for a long time, but at last he said, "All right, Oliver, I'll ask if they'll do it. The dance is tomorrow night at Edward's barn. I'll leave the fiddle here, and if I don't come back to pick it up, then you got to come to the dance and fiddle for us. I got your promise."

Oliver smiled under his dishcloth. They'd be fools to agree to that. You can't have any fun with a dishcloth over your head.

"So long, Oliver," Jim said. Oliver didn't answer. Jim went back on down the hill.

Oliver took the dishcloth off. The fiddle was laying in the light of the open door. He sucked a whisker and looked at it. Oliver knew the fiddle, and it was a good fiddle. He wondered if it was in tune and wanted to pick it up, but he let it lay there. His foot was tapping, and he slapped his knee to make it stop. He laughed to himself and muttered, "Them donkeys—what do they know?" Then he got up and moved around the little house on his dreary business.

The sun went down and the shadow of the fiddle case stretched across the floor. Oliver's eyes kept landing on the fiddle, and he stepped over the shadow when he crossed that way. It looked to him like the bow had new horsehair on it. But it didn't make any difference to him. He figured he'd never be playing on that fiddle, and he never touched it.

Next morning Oliver watched down the hill for Jim to come and tell him the deal was off and to get the fiddle. Noon came. Oliver ate some beans. Afternoon came on. Jim didn't show. Oliver began to get mad. He was mad that he had ever made the promise. It started to get dark. "Those cluckheads!" Oliver said, pulling the window shut. "They can't dance with dishcloths on their heads, or drink punch, either. They'll have a rotten time."

But a promise is a promise.

Finally he decided it was time to put his hat and coat on. "They tricked me," Oliver grumbled, "but I got a trick for them, too. They'll be sorry I came to their party." It wasn't a great trick Oliver had in mind, but just a miserable little one to make sure nobody could have any fun while he was there. He figured they'd ask him to leave shortly. He wouldn't even bother to take off his hat and coat.

He headed down the hill with the fiddle and into the little town. He entered Edward's barn with his hat pulled down and his collar turned up. It was dark except for two bare, hanging light bulbs, one over the center of the barn and one at the end where a sort of stage was built up. Oliver had played at shindigs there many times. He kept his head down, and only from the corners of his eyes could he see all the people sitting around the walls. "Lord, it's awfully dark," Oliver thought to himself, "and quiet. I figure they know that's the way I like it." He got under the light bulb that hung over the stage and took out the fiddle.

He tuned down to a fretful and lonesome sound, and then he played.

Of course, he knew they were all looking for happy dancing tunes, so first off he played a slow and sad tune about a man who was walking down a long road that had no ending and was gray all about, and the man was looking forward to being dead because it might be more cheerful. Nobody danced, naturally, and didn't clap either when Oliver finished it. "That's just right," Oliver thought. "I'll give them a wretched time." And he started on another.

The second tune he played was even slower and sadder, about a man who thought his heart was a pincushion and it seemed to him that everyone was sticking pins and needles into it, and it was hurtful even to listen to it. Nobody danced, and nobody even moved to the punch bowl to get their spirits up. "Now they're sorry I came," Oliver thought. Still, he had played that last tune especially sweet, and he expected someone might have clapped a little just for that, even if it was sad.

Oliver looked out a little under his hat as he retuned a bit. He tried to see Jim. He ought to come up and say hello at least, not just let him stand there completely alone. And he wondered where the other musicians were. Four people were sitting down off to the right of the stage. That would be them. Oliver considered it would be nice to have a little slide guitar on these slow ones, sort of mournful played, and a mouth harp and mandolin would fit in nice. "Naw! This is just the way I want it. One more gloomy song, and they'll ask me to leave."

So then he played another, this one about a man who had a wife that just recently moved to heaven, and how roses grew all over her tombstone even in the winter. Oliver was halfway through that before he remembered that he'd played that tune at his own wedding party. He pulled up short a bit then, but kept on playing it out, and a tear rolled down his cheek. Well, nobody could see. He wiped his eyes when he was finished.

Nobody clapped and nobody moved, just sat against the dark walls perfectly still. Among the dark figures was a lighter shape. Probably the bride in her white gown. Oliver remembered how lovely and happy his bride had been, and he felt a little mean when he thought about that, giving out such sad tunes.

He spoke out loud, the first words that were spoken since he came in. "Well, I guess you're all ready for me to leave now, and I will. But first I want to play just one happy tune for the bride, and so you can dance, and then I'll go." Then he did play a happy one, a fast one, carrying on with fiddling lively enough to scramble eggs. But nobody got up to dance, and when he was finished nobody moved or made a sound.

"Look here," Oliver said. "I reckon you can't dance with those dishcloths over your heads, I forgot about that. So take 'em off. I'll give you another dancing tune, then I'll go." And then he went into another, as sweet and light and fast as anyone ever could, something to get even a rock up and dancing, but nobody moved. And when he was finished they all sat silent with the dishcloths still on their heads.

"Come on," Oliver said. "Take those things off your heads. You other fellows get up here with your music and help me out. Let's have some dancing, drink some punch, let's get alive now." He stomped his foot three times and threw into a tune that would churn butter all by itself. But the other four musicians sat perfectly still, and so did everybody else, and Oliver was standing there under the light bulb in silence when he finished the tune.

He stood there with his head down, understanding things, and how it felt to be on the other side of the darkness and silence when all you wanted was some sign of life to help out. Then he leaned over and put the fiddle in the case and closed it. He said one last thing, then walked out from under the light toward the door. "Okay," he said. "That's a hard lesson, but I got it."

When he opened the door he bumped into someone sitting next to it against the wall, and the fellow fell off his chair. Oliver put a hand down to help him up. But the fellow just lay there. Oliver touched him. "What's this?" He felt around, then shoved back his hat for a look. It was a sack of grain he'd knocked over. And the next person sitting there was a sack of grain, too. And the next was a bale of hay.

Oliver walked completely around the barn. All the people were sacks of grain and bales of hay sitting against the dark walls, and the bride was a white sack of flour. The four musicians sitting off to the right of the stage were four old saddles setting on a rail.

When Oliver came around to the door again he heard music. He stepped outside and looked down the street. A barn down near the end was all lit up, and lots of people were moving about. He went back up on the stage, got the fiddle, and headed down the street.

Jim was standing by the door. "Waiting for you, Oliver," he said. "We're just getting under way—come on in." When he led Oliver inside everyone became quiet, first one little group of people then another, until at last everyone was silent and looking at Oliver. The bride and groom were holding hands. Jim made a motion and everyone headed for a chair against the walls. They all took out dishcloths to put over their heads.

"Edward's got himself a new barn, huh?" Oliver said.

"Yeah," said Jim. "I guess you didn't know that. Uses the old one to store stuff. I shoulda told you."

"It's all right," Oliver said. He looked up on the stage. Four musicians were sitting there with dishcloths over their heads. Then Jim took out a large dishcloth. Oliver touched him on the arm.

"Never mind that. And everyone else, too. Just be regular and dance. I'll fiddle for you."

Jim slapped him on the back and shouted out the good news. Oliver went up on the stage. Someone got him a mug of punch. The musicians tuned up. Oliver took off his hat and dropped it, and tossed his coat on a chair. They lit into a fast, happy tune. They danced and played and sang half the night.

Ah, they had a wonderful time. Oliver included.

THE HUNDRED-DOLLAR BILL

Rose Wilder Lane

This true story is told by Rose Wilder Lane, the daughter of Laura Ingalls Wilder, who wrote the Little House *series of books. Rose describes an incident that happened during her family's move from De Smet, South Dakota, to the "Land of the Big Red Apple" in Missouri. The Wilders traveled with their friends the Cooleys, whose sons Paul and George were slightly older than Rose, who was seven at the time.*

My mother had saved one hundred dollars to take to the Land of the Big Red Apple. All those dollars were one piece of paper, named "a hundred-dollar bill." She hid it in her writing desk, a fascinating wooden box which my father had made and polished so shiny smooth that stroking it was rapture. It opened on little brass hinges to lie spread flat and be a slanting green felt

surface to write on. At the top was a darling wooden tray
to hold my mother's pearl-handled pen, and beside this
was an inkwell. And the green felt was on a lid that lifted
up on tinier hinges to reveal the place for writing paper
underneath it. I was allowed to see and touch the desk
only when my mother opened it.

The hundred-dollar bill was a secret. My mother
locked it in the desk. Mr. and Mrs. Cooley knew, perhaps
Paul and George did, but we must not talk about it. I
must never, never, speak one word about that hundred-
dollar bill, not to anyone. Never, no matter what
happened.

◆　◆　◆

I do not remember how many days my father spent
hunting for land that the secret hundred-dollar bill
would buy. Every morning he rode away with some land
agent to limp up and down the hills and to come back at
evening, nothing found yet.

Paul and George and I were joyous. After the long
boredom of so many dull days that we hardly
remembered De Smet, now every day was Sunday
without Sunday's clean clothes and staid behavior. The
camp was a Sunday camp; the Cooleys' wagons on one
side, ours on the other; in the grove between them the
table and chairs were set and the hammock hung in the
shade. The camp stove stood a little way apart over
cooling ashes. Farther away the horses were tied under

the trees, and behind the wagons were screened places for our Saturday baths.

We must stay within sight or at least within hearing if our mothers called us, but as soon as morning tasks were done, we were free to play in the woods. All day we climbed trees, picked berries, ate unripe walnuts and hazel nuts, cracked between two stones. We startled rabbits that we must not chase far; we watched squirrels and birds, beetles and anthills. The hot air was full of good smells of rotting logs, dusty weeds, damp underneaths of mats of last year's oak leaves. Dandelion stems curled bitter on my tongue's tip, and the green curls wilted over my ears.

Sharp flat stones were thick underfoot; we stubbed our toes on them, and all our big toes were wrapped in rags. Stone bruises on our summer-calloused heels didn't stop our running. We found toadstools and mosses like teeny-tiniest forests, flat greenish gray lichen on rocks, little perfect skins of locusts, empty, thin, and brittle, clinging with tiny claws to the bark of trees.

We picked up strange stones. When I showed my father a thin triangular one, wavy all over and sharp pointed, he said it was an Indian arrowhead. We collected dozens of them, and Paul found a stone ax head.

One day I had to stay in camp with Mrs. Cooley; I must mind her and not go out of her sight. My father had found a place, my mother was going with him to see it, and they wanted no worry about me while they were gone. There never had been such a long morning. I was embarrassed and so was Mrs. Cooley. When at last I saw the team coming, my father and mother coming back, I felt like exploding; I could hardly be still and not speak until spoken to.

My father was glowing and my mother shining. She never had talked so fast. Just what they wanted, she told Mrs. Cooley; so much, much more than they'd hoped for. A year-round spring of the best water you ever drank, a snug log house, in woods, on a hill, only a mile and a half from town so Rose could walk to school, and to cap all— just think!—four hundred young apple trees, heeled in, all ready to set out when the land was cleared. They'd bought it; as soon as dinner was over they were going to the bank to sign the papers. We were moving out that afternoon.

When he was excited, my father always held himself quiet and steady, moving and speaking with deliberation. Sometimes my quick mother flew out at him, but this day she was soft and warm. She left him eating at the camp table, told me to clear it and wash the dishes when he was through, and went into the screened place to get ready to meet the banker.

I perched on a stump and watched her brush out her hair and braid it. She had beautiful hair, roan brown, very fine and thick. Unbraided, it shimmered down to her heels; it was so long that when it was tightly braided she could sit on the braids. Usually it hung down her back in one wide braid, but when she dressed up she must put up her hair and endure the headache.

Now she wound the braid around and around into a big mass on the back of her head, and fastened it with her tortoise-shell pins. She fluffed her bangs into a soft little mat in front, watching her comb in the small looking glass fastened to a tree, and suddenly I realized that she was whistling; I remembered that I hadn't heard her whistling lately.

"Whistling girls and crowing hens always come to some bad ends," she'd say gaily. She was whistling always. She whistled like a bird whistling a tune, clear and soft, clear and sweet, trilling, chirping, or dropping notes one by one as a meadowlark drops them from the sky. I was pleased to hear her whistling again.

Whistling, she buttoned up her new shoes with the buttonhook. She took off her calico dress and folded it neatly. Standing in her bleached muslin petticoats and corset cover trimmed with crocheted lace, she took her best dress, her black cloth wedding dress, out of the box in which it had traveled from Dakota. Whistling O Susanna, don't you cry for me, she put on the skirt and smoothed the placket. I was sorry that the skirt hid her new shoes. She coaxed her arms into the basque's tight sleeves and carefully buttoned all the glittery jet buttons up its front to her chin. With her gold pin she pinned the fold of ribbon, robin's-egg blue, to the front of the stand-up collar. Then, the very last thing, the climax: she pinned on her black sailor hat with the blue ribbon around the crown and the spray of wheat standing straight up at one side. The braids in back tilted the hat forward just a little; in front, the narrow brim rested on the mat of bangs.

She looked lovely; she was beautiful. You could see my father think so, when she came out and he looked at her.

61

She told him to hurry or they'd be late, but she spoke as if she were singing, not cross at all. He went into the screened place to change his shirt and comb his hair and mustache, and put on his new hat. To me my mother said that I could clear the table now, be sure to wash every dish while they were gone, and, as usual, she told me to be careful not to break one. I never had broken a dish.

I remember all this so clearly because of what happened. I had taken away the dishes and wiped the table. My mother put down on it her clean handkerchief and her little red cloth pocketbook with the mother-of-pearl sides; she was wearing her kid gloves. Carefully she brought the writing desk and set it on the table. She laid back its slanted upper half and lifted out the narrow wooden tray that held the pen and the inkwell.

The hundred-dollar bill was gone.

There was a shock, like stepping in the dark on a top step that isn't there. But it could not be true. It was true; the place in the desk was empty. Everything changed. In the tight strangeness my father and mother were not like them; I did not feel like me.

They asked, Had I told someone? No. Had I never said anything to anyone, ever, about that money? No. Had I seen a stranger near the wagon when they were not there? No. Or in camp? No.

My mother said it wasn't possible; not the Cooleys. My father agreed, no, not them. It *must* be there. My mother had seen it last in Kansas.

They took every sheet of writing paper out of the desk and shook it; they took each letter out of its envelope, unfolded it, looked into the empty envelope. They turned the desk upside down and shook it, the felt-covered inside lids flapping. My mother said they were losing their senses. Suddenly she thought, hoped, asked, Had I taken it myself, to play with?

NO! I felt scalded. She asked, Was I sure? I hadn't just opened the desk sometime, for fun? My throat swelled shut; I shook my head, no. "Don't cry," she said automatically. I wouldn't cry, I never cried, I was angry, insulted, miserable, I was not a baby who'd play with money or open that desk for fun, I was going on eight years old. I was little, alone, and scared. My father and mother sat there, still. In the long stillness I sank slowly into nothing but terror, pure terror without cause or object, a nightmare terror.

Finally my mother said, "Well." She meant, No use crying over spilled milk. What can't be cured must be endured. My father told her not to blame herself, it wasn't her fault. Carefully she peeled off her thin kid gloves. She turned them right-side-out finger by finger, smoothed them. She said that he'd better go explain to the banker.

Somehow the worst was over when he tried to put it off, saying something might turn up, and she flared out that he knew as well as she did, "nothing turns up that we don't turn up ourselves." Then she told me to run away and play, and I remembered the unwashed dishes. She had forgotten them.

For days, I don't remember how many days, everything was the same as ever and not at all the same. I said nothing about the disaster; I didn't want to. My mother told Mrs. Cooley that they thought best to take time to make up their minds. My father looked for work in town. My mother knew nobody there. Mr. Cooley sold one of his teams and one wagon; and Paul and George were going to move into the hotel and help run it. I knew we could sell the horses, but what then? Covered wagons were going by every day, going both ways as usual, some camping overnight nearby. Often I tried to think what would happen when we had nothing to eat; I couldn't.

Blackberries were fewer now and smaller. I was deep in the briary patch, hunting them, when my mother called, and called again before I could get out without tearing my dress on the clutching thorns and run over the sharp stones to the camp. My father was hitching up, my mother was putting last things into the wagon. They had bought the farm. She had found the hundred-dollar bill. In the writing desk. The jolting had slipped it into a crack in the desk, and I was to stop asking questions and get into the wagon. Just as she was, my mother had found my father and gone to sign the papers, and just as I was, without even washing my feet, I was to obey her and get up onto that wagon seat, *now*, and no more words about it.

THE INVISIBLE CHILD

Tove Jansson

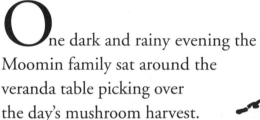

One dark and rainy evening the Moomin family sat around the veranda table picking over the day's mushroom harvest. The big table was covered with newspapers, and in the center of it stood the lighted kerosene lamp. But the corners of the veranda were dark.

"My has been picking pepper spunk again," Moominpappa said. "Last year she collected flybane."

"Let's hope she takes to chanterelles next autumn," said Moominmamma. "Or at least to something not directly poisonous."

"Hope for the best and prepare for the worst," little My observed with a chuckle.

They continued their work in peaceful silence.

Suddenly, there were a few light taps on the glass pane in the door, and without waiting for an answer Too-ticky came in and shook the rain off her oilskin jacket. Then she held the door open and called out in the dark, "Well, come along!"

"Whom are you bringing?" Moomintroll asked.

"It's Ninny," Too-ticky said. "Yes, her name's Ninny."

She still held the door open, waiting. No one came.

"Oh, well," Too-ticky said and shrugged her shoulders. "If she's too shy she'd better stay there for a while."

"She'll be drenched through," said Moominmamma.

"Perhaps that won't matter much when one's invisible," Too-ticky said and sat down by the table. The family stopped working and waited for an explanation.

"You all know, don't you, that if people are frightened very often, they sometimes become invisible," Too-ticky said and swallowed a small egg mushroom that looked like a little snowball. "Well. This Ninny was frightened the wrong way by a lady who had taken care of her without really liking her. I've met this lady, and she was horrid. Not the angry sort, you know, which would have been understandable. No, she was the icily ironical kind."

"What's ironical?" Moomintroll asked.

"Well, imagine that you slip on a rotten mushroom and sit down on the basket of newly picked ones," Too-ticky said. "The natural thing for your mother would be to be angry. But no, she isn't. Instead she says, very coldly, 'I understand that's your idea of a graceful dance, but I'd thank you not to do it in people's food.' Something like that."

"How unpleasant," Moomintroll said.

"Yes, isn't it," replied Too-ticky. "This was the way this lady used to talk. She was ironic all day long every day, and finally the kid started to turn pale and fade around the edges, and less and less was seen of her. Last Friday one couldn't catch sight of her at all. The lady gave her away to me and said she really couldn't take care of relatives she couldn't see."

"And what did you do to the lady?" My asked with bulging eyes. "Did you bash her head?"

"That's of no use with the ironic sort," Too-ticky said. "I took Ninny home with me, of course. And now I've brought her here for you to make her visible again."

There was a slight pause. Only the rain was heard, rustling along over the veranda roof. Everybody stared at Too-ticky and thought for a while.

"Does she talk?" Moominpappa asked.

"No. But the lady has hung a small silver bell around her neck so that one can hear where she is."

Too-ticky arose and opened the door again. "Ninny!" she called out in the dark.

The cool smell of autumn crept in
from the garden, and a square of light
threw itself on the wet grass. After a
while there was a slight tinkle outside,
rather hesitantly. The sound came
up the steps and stopped. A bit above
the floor a small silver bell was seen
hanging in the air on a black ribbon.
Ninny seemed to have a very thin neck.

"All right," Too-ticky said. "Now,
here's your new family. They're a bit silly at times,
but rather decent, largely speaking."

"Give the kid a chair," Moominpappa said. "Does she
know how to pick mushrooms?"

"I really know nothing at all about Ninny," Too-ticky
said. "I've only brought her here and told you what I
know. Now I have a few other things to attend to. Please
look in some day, won't you, and let me know how you
get along. Cheerio."

When Too-ticky had gone the family sat quite silent,
looking at the empty chair and the silver bell. After a
while one of the chanterelles slowly rose from the heap
on the table. Invisible paws picked it clean from needles
and earth. Then it was cut to pieces, and the pieces
drifted away and laid themselves in the basin. Another
mushroom sailed up from the table.

"Thrilling!" My said with awe. "Try to give her
something to eat. I'd like to know if you can see the food
when she swallows it."

"How on earth does one make her visible again?" Moominpappa said worriedly. "Should we take her to a doctor?"

"I don't think so," said Moominmamma. "I believe she wants to be invisible for a while. Too-ticky said she's shy. Better leave the kid alone until something turns up."

And so it was decided.

The eastern attic room happened to be unoccupied, so Moominmamma made Ninny a bed there. The silver bell tinkled along after her upstairs and reminded Moominmamma of the cat that once had lived with them. At the bedside she laid out the apple, the glass of juice, and the three striped pieces of candy everybody in the house was given at bedtime.

Then she lighted a candle and said:

"Now have a good sleep, Ninny. Sleep as late as you can. There'll be tea for you in the morning any time you want. And if you happen to get a funny feeling or if you want anything, just come downstairs and tinkle."

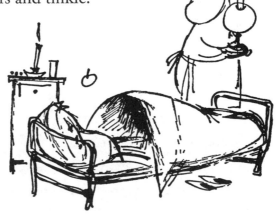

Moominmamma saw the quilt raise itself to form a very small mound. A dent appeared in the pillow. She went downstairs again to her own room and started looking through Granny's old notes about Infallible Household Remedies. Evil Eye. Melancholy. Colds. No. There didn't seem to be anything suitable. Yes, there was. Toward the end of the notebook she found a few lines written down at the time when Granny's hand was already rather shaky. "If people start getting misty and difficult to see." Good. Moominmamma read the recipe, which was rather complicated, and started at once to mix the medicine for little Ninny.

The bell came tinkling downstairs, one step at a time, with a small pause between each step. Moomintroll had waited for it all morning. But the silver bell wasn't the exciting thing. That was the paws. Ninny's paws were coming down the steps. They were very small, with anxiously bunched toes. Nothing else of Ninny was visible. It was very odd.

Moomintroll drew back behind the porcelain stove and stared bewitchedly at the paws that passed him on their way to the veranda. Now she served herself some tea. The cup was raised in the air and sank back again. She ate some bread and butter and marmalade. Then the cup and saucer drifted away to the kitchen, were washed and put away in the closet. You see, Ninny was a very orderly little child.

Moomintroll rushed out in the garden and shouted, "Mamma! She's got paws! You can see her paws!"

I thought as much, Moominmamma was thinking where she sat high in the apple tree. Granny knew a thing or two. Now when the medicine starts to work we'll be on the right way.

"Splendid," said Moominpappa. "And better still when she shows her snout one day. It makes me feel sad to talk with people who are invisible. And who never answer me."

"Hush, dear," Moominmamma said warningly. Ninny's paws were standing in the grass among the fallen apples.

"Hello Ninny," shouted My. "You've slept like a hog. When are you going to show your snout? You must look a fright if you've wanted to be invisible."

"Shut up," Moomintroll whispered, "she'll be hurt." He went running up to Ninny and said:

"Never mind My. She's hard-boiled. You're really safe here among us. Don't even think about that horrid lady. She can't come here and take you away. . . ."

In a moment Ninny's paws had faded away and become nearly indistinguishable from the grass.

"Darling, you're an ass," said Moominmamma. "You can't go about reminding the kid about those things. Now pick apples and don't talk rubbish."

They all picked apples.

After a while Ninny's paws became clearer again and climbed one of the trees.

It was a beautiful autumn morning. The shadows made one's snout a little chilly but the sunshine felt nearly like summer. Everything was wet from the night's rain, and all colors were strong and clear. When all the apples were picked or shaken down, Moominpappa carried the biggest apple mincer out in the garden, and they started making apple-cheese.

Moomintroll turned the handle, Moominmamma fed the mincer with apples, and Moominpappa carried the filled jars to the veranda. Little My sat in a tree singing the Big Apple Song.

Suddenly there was a crash.

On the garden path appeared a large heap of apple-cheese, all prickly with glass splinters. Beside the heap one could see Ninny's paws, rapidly fading away.

"Oh," said Moominmamma. "That was the jar we use to give to the bumblebees. Now we needn't carry it down to the field. And Granny always said that if you want the earth to grow something for you, then you have to give it a present in the autumn."

Ninny's paws appeared back again, and above them a pair of spindly legs came to view. Above the legs one could see the faint outline of a brown dress hem.

"I can see her legs!" cried Moomintroll.

"Congrats," said little My, looking down out of her tree. "Not bad. But the Groke knows why you must wear snuff-brown."

Moominmamma nodded to herself and sent a thought to her Granny and the medicine.

Ninny padded along after them all day. They became used to the tinkle and no longer thought Ninny very remarkable.

By evening they had nearly forgotten about her. But when everybody was in bed Moominmamma took out a rose-pink shawl of hers and made it into a little dress. When it was ready she carried it upstairs to the eastern attic room and cautiously laid it out on a chair. Then she made a broad hair ribbon out of the material left over.

Moominmamma was enjoying herself tremendously. It was exactly like sewing doll's clothes again. And the funny thing was that one didn't know if the doll had yellow or black hair.

The following day Ninny had her dress on. She was visible up to her neck, and when she came down to morning tea she bobbed and piped:

"Thank you all ever so much."

The family felt very embarrassed, and no one found anything to say. Also it was hard to know where to look when one talked to Ninny. Of course, one tried to look a bit above the bell where Ninny was supposed to have her eyes. But then very easily one found oneself staring at some of the visible things further down instead, and it gave one an impolite feeling.

Moominpappa cleared his throat. "We're happy to see," he started, "that we see more of Ninny today. The more we see the happier we are. . . ."

My gave a laugh and banged the table with her spoon. "Fine that you've started talking," she said. "Hope you have anything to say. Do you know any good games?"

"No," Ninny piped. "But I've heard about games."

Moomintroll was delighted. He decided to teach Ninny all the games he knew.

After coffee all three of them went down to the river to play. Only Ninny turned out to be quite impossible. She bobbed and nodded and very seriously replied, quite, and how funny, and of course, but it was clear to all that she played only from politeness and not to have fun.

"Run, run, can't you!" My cried. "Or can't you even jump?"

Ninny's thin legs dutifully ran and jumped. Then she stood still again with arms dangling. The empty dress neck over the bell was looking strangely helpless.

"D'you think anybody likes that?" My cried. "Haven't you any life in you? D'you want a biff on the nose?"

"Rather not," Ninny piped humbly.

"She can't play," mumbled Moomintroll.

"She can't get angry," little My said. "That's what's wrong with her. Listen, you," My continued and went close to Ninny with a menacing look. "You'll never have a face of your own until you've learned to fight. Believe me."

"Yes, of course," Ninny replied, cautiously backing away.

There was no further turn for the better.

At last they stopped trying to teach Ninny to play. She didn't like funny stories either. She never laughed at the right places. She never laughed at all, in fact. This had a depressing effect on the person who told the story. And she was left alone to herself.

Days went by, and Ninny was still without a face. They became accustomed to seeing her pink dress marching along behind Moominmamma. As soon as Moominmamma stopped, the silver bell also stopped, and when she continued her way the bell began tinkling again. A bit above the dress a big rose-pink bow was bobbing in thin air.

Moominmamma continued to treat Ninny with Granny's medicine, but nothing further happened. So after some time she stopped the treatment, thinking that many people had managed all right before without a head, and besides perhaps Ninny wasn't very good-looking.

Now everyone could imagine for himself what she looked like, and this can often brighten up a relationship.

One day the family went off through the wood down to the beach. They were going to pull the boat up for winter. Ninny came tinkling behind as usual, but when they came in view of the sea she suddenly stopped. Then she lay down on her stomach in the sand and started to whine.

"What's come over Ninny? Is she frightened?" asked Moominpappa.

"Perhaps she hasn't seen the sea before," Moominmamma said. She stooped and exchanged a few whispering words with Ninny. Then she straightened up again and said:

"No, it's the first time. Ninny thinks the sea's too big."

"Of all the silly kids," little My started, but Moominmamma gave her a severe look and said, "Don't be a silly kid yourself. Now let's pull the boat ashore."

They went out on the landing stage to the bathing hut where Too-ticky lived, and knocked at the door.

"Hullo," Too-ticky said, "how's the invisible child?"

"There's only her snout left," Moominpappa replied. "At the moment she's a bit startled but it'll pass over. Can you lend us a hand with the boat?"

"Certainly," Too-ticky said.

While the boat was pulled ashore and turned keel upward Ninny had padded down to the water's edge and was standing immobile on the wet sand. They left her alone.

Moominmamma sat down on the landing stage and looked down into the water. "Dear me, how cold it looks," she said. And then she yawned a bit and added that nothing exciting had happened for weeks.

Moominpappa gave Moomintroll a wink, pulled a horrible face, and started to steal up to Moominmamma from behind.

Of course, he didn't really think of pushing her in the water as he had done so many times when she was young. Perhaps he didn't even want to startle her, but just to amuse the kids a little.

But before he reached her a sharp cry was heard, a pink streak of lightning shot over the landing stage, and Moominpappa let out a scream and dropped his hat into the water. Ninny had sunk her small invisible teeth in Moominpappa's tail, and they were sharp.

"Good work!" cried My. "I couldn't have done it better myself!"

Ninny was standing on the landing stage. She had a small, snub-nosed, angry face below a red tangle of hair. She was hissing at Moominpappa like a cat.

"Don't you *dare* push her into the big horrible sea!" she cried.

"I see her, I see her!" shouted Moomintroll. "She's sweet!"

"Sweet my eye," said Moominpappa, inspecting his bitten tail. "She's the silliest, nastiest, badly-brought-uppest child I've ever seen, with or without a head."

He knelt down on the landing stage and tried to fish for his hat with a stick. And in some mysterious way he managed to tip himself over, and tumbled in on his head.

He came up at once, standing safely on the bottom, with his snout above water and his ears filled with mud.

"Oh dear!" Ninny was shouting. "Oh, how great! Oh, how funny!"

The landing stage shook with her laughter.

"I believe she's never laughed before," Too-ticky said wonderingly. "You seem to have changed her; she's even worse than little My. But the main thing is that one can see her, of course."

"It's all thanks to Granny," Moominmamma said.

IN THE TIME OF THE DRUMS

*Gullah folktale
as told by Kim L. Siegelson*

In the long ago time before now, on an island fringed by marsh meadows and washed by ocean tides, men and women and their children lived enslaved. This was the time when giant live oaks trembled with the sound of drums, and, say some, it was a time when people could walk beneath the water.

Used to be, in those early days, ships as big as barns would land at a dock on a bluff near Teakettle Creek: pirate ships with treasure to bury, cargo ships filled with cinnamon, slave ships bringing African people to do work on plantation farms.

Some of those Africans came knowing how to carve wood and make sweet-grass baskets and goatskin drums. With those things they reminded themselves of home. Wished to go back there.

One boy, name of Mentu, had never known Africa or longed for it. He was an island-born boy.

Mentu could scoot to the top of a live oak faster than a brush-tail squirrel. Could lift a black iron skillet above his head with one hand, even though he still wore shirttails. "Look how strong I am!" he would say to his grandmother, Twi.

Twi would smile back and cluck her tongue at him. "Stop your foolin' lest the overseer catch you, sir. Your time for strong will come soon enough."

"When?" Mentu would ask. Twi would not say.

Mentu had always lived with Twi. The islanders, black and white, all feared her.

Africa had been her birthplace.

There, she had learned powerful root magic at her own grandmother's knee. "Ibo conjure woman," the islanders called her "Older than anyone living," they said. But Mentu paid them no mind, had only known kindness from Twi. You see, Twi loved Mentu like her own soul. Like the faraway rivers and mountains of her native land. Some said his first breath had come from her own mouth. That as a new babe he had been still until she whispered the secret of life onto his tongue. He had wailed at the truth of it and waved his fists at her, and at the charm bag she held out to him. "Not with fists," she had said, gathering him against her chest. "Listen close and learn how to be strong." He had slept to the sound of Twi's heart.

Every day Mentu went with Twi to take water to the fields. Could carry two full buckets by himself. Strong as that made him seem, he was a mischief-making boy-child all the same.

"The bucket handles pinch my hands" he sometimes complained to Twi. "You carry the water for me today."

"Nawsir!" she would say and cluck her tongue. "Twi can't be taking up your burden from you. Look out to the field workers when your hands is aching and count your luck. Soon it will be your time to be strong-strong, and Twi won't be helping you then."

"How will I know when to be strong-strong if you don't tell me?" Mentu asked.

Twi still would not answer She knew many secrets. She shared only what she wanted.

Mentu looked to the fields and watched the people bend beneath the blistering sun to slave in soil planted with cotton and cane and blue indigo seed. Saw how they worked from dark of morning to dark of night, harvesting what they could not keep.

Twi told him that the long, hard work had broken them. Made memories of Africa sink so far back in their minds that they could no longer be reached. The old ways had slowly slipped away, and been left behind like sweat drops in a newly plowed row.

But Twi remembered the time before.

Spoke the old words to herself in the morning while she worked. Sang African songs to Mentu in the afternoon until he could sing them back. At dinner, told him stories so rich that he could almost smell the sweet-scented air of her homeland. Put the skin drum between her own knees and taught him ancient rhythms until they felt as natural to him as his own heart beating.

Then, come a day so hot even the gnats hushed their whining to sit among the tree shadows. In that breathless quiet, Mentu and Twi filled their buckets with well water. But before they could carry them to the fields they heard the sound of drums beating from the far end of the island. *Bop-boom-boom*! *Bop-boom-boom*! It was a message in rhythm that meant "A ship is come! A ship is come!"

Mentu beat his own drum. *Be-e-bow. Be-e-bow.* "We hear. We hear." He and Twi gathered with everyone else at the bluff to see what the ship had brought. It flew a Spanish flag, but it did not carry gold or jewels or sweet spices from India. The ship held a whole village of Ibo people from the African kingdom of Benin. They had been captured by the ship's owners and brought to the island to be sold.

Their ride across the ocean passage had been long, with many days spent in airless dark beneath the pitching decks of the ship.

When the ship docked at the bluff, the Ibo people could no longer hear the crash of ocean waves—only the groan of the ship, the flapping sails, and their own harsh breathing. They trembled and waited quietly, listening to learn something of their fate. Through the wooden side of the ship came the sound of the island drums. The music of Africa.

"Has some magic brought us home?" they cried. They drummed an answer using their feet on the wooden floor.

Mentu heard the rumble of their pounding feet, and it spoke to him like the beating of his heart. "We are home! We are home!" the people drummed. But they were far from home.

Mentu and Twi watched the Ibo people brought up from the dark hull of the ship into the light. Saw how they squinted into the sun. How they looked out over the unfamiliar marsh meadows in despair. The ship had not returned them to Africa. Would never take them home again.

Try as the ship's captain might to make them move, the Ibo refused to set a foot on the island. Mentu turned away when the overseer lashed them with his whip. But the people would not budge for the whip, just joined their hands tight together and began to chant a song in their own language.

Mentu listened as though his soul lived in his ears. He heard Twi's music in their song. Old words from the place where she had been born.

"What are they saying, Twi?" he asked. "Sounds like magic."

Twi's eyes glittered like moonsparkle on dark water. "Old magic long forgot, boy," she whispered. "The people want to go home. Say the water brought 'em cross the passage and it can take 'em back, fe true." She hung her charm bag around Mentu's neck. "That water can take me on, too, Mentu. You are old enough. Your time to be strong-strong is near."

Mentu began to tremble. "Will the water take me, Twi? I want to go with you."

His grandmother shook her head. "Water won't take you. You was born here. Won't take the others 'cause they've forgot too much."

"But you haven't taught me all your secrets, Twi," Mentu cried. "You haven't told me when my time will come yet."

Twi clucked her tongue at him, still a mischief-making boy-child. "Twi has taught you many things, Mentu. More secrets than you think. But I will tell you one more. Your time to be strong-strong will come when your back is bent in the fields and your hands are stuck full of cotton spurs. Because then the old ways will try to grow weak inside you. Don't let 'em! Takes a mighty strength not to forget who you are. Where you come from. To help others remember it, too. Now I must leave you, my child, my heart."

Then Twi kissed Mentu fast as a dragonfly. Took off running. And as she ran, the years melted from her like butter on an ash cake. Her back drew up straight. Her hair grew dark and thick with braids, and her skin smoothed until she looked like the young woman who had been taken from Africa those many years before. The islanders feared Twi more than ever when they saw this happen, and they fell back to let her pass. No one tried to stop her.

From the bluff she held her hands out to the Ibo people on the dock and spoke to them. "Come with me, my brothers and sisters. I will take you home."

Mentu wept as the people crossed the dock to join the young Twi on the land. The slave catchers tried to slip ropes around their necks and arms to hold them back, but couldn't. The ropes slipped through flesh and bone like it was smoke and seawater.

Twi clasped hands with the Ibo people and led them down the bluff to the water's edge. "Twi!" Mentu called out to her, but she would not turn back, even for him.

She chanted as she led the people waist deep into the waters of Teakettle Creek. Mentu wiped away his tears and chanted with her in a voice as strong as he could make it, "The water can take us home. The water can take us home." He tried to run to her but found his feet fastened to the land so that he could not move.

Twi and the other Ibo people lifted their faces to the sky as water crept over their shoulders and then their necks. But they kept walking, as their chains snapped away. "The water can take us home," they sang. "It can take us home."

Their song dissolved into bubble and foam as Teakettle Creek swirled over the tops of their heads. Mentu's feet suddenly pulled away from the ground and he ran to the water, but he couldn't see Twi or the Ibo people beneath its surface.

In time, Mentu swore to everyone left behind that Twi and the Ibos had walked all the way back to Africa on the bottom of the ocean, pulling each other along the sandy floors, pushing aside seaweed like long grass.

"But their chains and their song will never leave Teakettle Creek," others said. "And the water there will always be salty as tears."

The islanders called that place Ibo's Landing. Stopped fishing there and never cast another net in Teakettle Creek for fear of pulling up those chains sunk deep in soft gray mud. Shivered when snowy egrets rose from the marsh grass like spirits in the evening.

As for Mentu, he learned to be strong-strong in the fields beneath the blistering sun, just as Twi had told him. He sang her old songs to himself while he worked and to his children until they could sing them back to him. He told stories so rich that they wondered if he had lived in Africa himself. And he played rhythms on the skin drum until they felt their own hearts beat in time. Gave them their own drums and they all played together, Mentu and his children.

And they taught their own children, and they taught theirs, through slave time and freedom time and on up until now time.

Fe true, it takes a mighty strength not to forget.

LEARNING THE GAME

Francisco Jiménez

I was in a bad mood. It was the last day of seventh grade before summer vacation. I had known the day was coming, but I had tried not to think about it because it made me sad. For my classmates, it was a happy day. During the afternoon, Miss Logan asked for volunteers to share what they were going to do during the summer; lots of hands went up. Some talked about going away on trips; others about summer camp. I folded my hands under the desk, lowered my head, and tried not to listen. After a while, I managed to tune out what they were saying and only heard faint voices coming from different parts of the room.

In the school bus on the way home, I took out my note pad and pencil from my shirt pocket and began figuring out how much time before I would start school again—from the middle of June until the first week of November, about four and a half months. Ten weeks picking strawberries in Santa Maria and another eight weeks harvesting grapes and cotton in Fresno. As I added the number of days, I started to get a headache. Looking out the window I said to myself, "One-hundred-thirty-two more days after tomorrow."

As soon as I arrived home, I took two of Papá's aspirins and lay down. I had just closed my eyes when I heard Carlos, our neighbor, shouting outside. "Come on, Panchito, we're starting the game."

The game was kick-the-can. I played it with Carlos and my younger brothers, Trampita, Torito, and Rubén, on school days when I had no homework, and on weekends when I was not too tired from working in the fields.

"Hurry, or else!" Carlos hollered impatiently.

I liked the game, but I did not enjoy playing with Carlos. He was older than I, and often reminded me of it, especially when I disagreed with him. If we wanted to play, we had to follow his rules. No one could play unless he said so. He wore tight jeans and a white T-shirt with the sleeves rolled up to show off his muscles. Under his right sleeve, he tucked a cigarette pack.

"Come on Panchito!" Trampita yelled. "You're making us wait."

I went outside to play. I wanted to forget about the next 133 days.

"It's about time," Carlos said, giving me a light punch on the right shoulder. "You'll be the guard," he said, pointing at Rubén. "Trampita, you draw the circle.

Torito, you get the can." As Carlos was giving orders, I saw Manuelito standing by one of the garbage cans. During every game, he stood by himself on the sidelines because Carlos would not let him play. "Let Manuelito be the guard," I said to Carlos.

"No way," he responded annoyingly. "I already told you before, he can't play. He's too slow."

"Come on, Carlos, let him play," I insisted.

"No!" he shouted, giving me and Manuelito a dirty look.

"Go ahead and play, Panchito," Manuelito said timidly. "I'll stand here and watch."

We started the game, and the more we played, the less I thought about my troubles. Even my headache went away. We played until dark.

The alarm clock went off early the next morning. I glanced at the window. It was still dark outside. I shut my eyes, trying to get one more minute of sleep, but Roberto, my older brother, jumped out of bed and pulled off the covers. "Time to get up!" he said. When I saw him putting on his work clothes, I remembered we were going to work, and not to school. My shoulders felt heavy.

On the way to the fields, Papá turned on the *Carcachita*'s headlights to see through the thick fog that blew in from the coast. It covered the valley every morning, like a large gray sheet. Ito, the sharecropper, was waiting for us when we arrived. Then a black pickup truck appeared. We could see it through the wall of fog, not far from where we parked. The driver stopped behind our *Carcachita* and, in perfect Spanish, ordered the passenger who rode in the bed of the truck to get off.

"Who's that?" I asked Papá, pointing to the driver.

"Don't point," Papá said. "It's bad manners. He's Mr. Díaz, the *contratista*. He runs the *bracero* camp for Sheehey Berry Farms. The man with him is one of the *braceros*."

In his broken Spanish, Ito introduced us to Gabriel, the man who accompanied the *contratista*.

Gabriel looked a few years older than Roberto. He wore a pair of loose tan pants and a blue shirt. The shirt was faded. His straw hat was slightly tilted to the right, and he had long dark sideburns that were trimmed and came down to the middle of his square jaw. His face was weather beaten. The deep cracks in the back of his heels were as black as the soles of his *huaraches*.

Gabriel took off his hat and we shook hands. He seemed nervous. But he relaxed when we greeted him in Spanish.

After the *contratista* left, we marched in line to the end of the field, selected a row, and started to work. Gabriel ended up between Papá and me. Because it was Gabriel's first time harvesting strawberries, Ito asked Papá to show him how to pick. "It's easy, Don Gabriel," Papá said. "The main thing is to make sure the strawberry is ripe and not bruised or rotten. And when you get tired from squatting, you can pick on your knees." Gabriel learned quickly by watching and following Papá.

90

At noon, Papá invited Gabriel to join us for lunch in our *Carcachita*. He sat next to me in the back seat while Roberto and Papá sat in the front. From his brown paper bag, he pulled out a Coke and three sandwiches: one of mayonnaise and two of jelly. "Not again! We get this same lunch from that Díaz every day," he complained. "I am really tired of this."

"You can have one of my *taquitos*," I said.

"Only if you take this jelly sandwich," he responded, handing it to me. I looked at Papá's face. When I saw him smile, I took it and thanked him.

"Do you have a family, Don Gabriel?" Papá asked.

"Yes, and I miss them a lot," he answered. "Especially my three kids."

"How old are they?" Papá asked.

"The oldest is five, the middle one is three, and the little one, a girl, is two."

"And you, Don Pancho, how many do you have?"

"A handful," Papá answered, grinning. "Five boys and a girl. All living at home."

"You're lucky. You get to see them every day," Gabriel said. "I haven't seen mine for months." He continued as though thinking out loud. "I didn't want to leave them, but I had no choice. We have to eat, you know. I send them a few dollars every month for food and things. I'd like to send them more, but after I pay Díaz for room and board and transportation, little is left." Then in an angry tone of voice he added, "Díaz is a crook. He overcharges for everything. That *sin vergüenza* doesn't know who he's dealing with."

At this point, we heard the honking of a car horn. It was Ito signaling us that it was time to go back to work. Our half-hour lunch break was over.

That evening, and for several days after, I was too tired to play outside when we got home from work. I went straight to bed after supper. But as I got more and more used to picking strawberries, I began to play kick-the-can again. The game was always the same. We played by Carlos's rules, and he refused to let Manuelito play.

Work was always the same, too. We picked from six o'clock in the morning until six in the afternoon. Even though the days were long, I looked forward to seeing Gabriel and having lunch with him every day. I enjoyed listening to him tell stories and talk about Mexico. He was as proud of being from the state of Morelos as my father was about being from Jalisco.

One Sunday, near the end of the strawberry season, Ito sent me to work for a sharecropper who was sick and needed extra help that day. His field was next to Ito's. Gabriel was loaned out to the same farmer. As soon as I arrived, the *contratista* began giving me orders. "Listen, *hüerquito*, I want you to hoe weeds. But first, give me and Gabriel a hand," he said. Gabriel and I climbed onto the bed of the truck and helped him unload a plow. The *contratista* tied one end of a thick rope to it and, handing the other end to Gabriel, said, "Here, tie this around your waist. I want you to till the furrows."

"I can't do that," Gabriel said with a painful look in his face.

"What do you mean you can't?" responded the *contratista*, placing his hands on his hips.

"In my country, oxen pull plows, not men," Gabriel replied, tilting his hat back. "I am not an animal."

The *contratista* walked up to Gabriel and yelled in his face, "Well this isn't your country, idiot! You either do what I say or I'll have you fired!"

"Don't do that, please," Gabriel said. "I have a family to feed."

"I don't give a damn about your family!" the *contratista* replied, grabbing Gabriel by the shirt collar and pushing him. Gabriel lost his balance and fell backward. As he hit the ground, the *contratista* kicked him in the side with the tip of his boot. Gabriel sprung up and, with both hands clenched, lunged at the *contratista*. White as a ghost, Díaz quickly jumped back. "Don't be stupid . . . your family," he stammered. Gabriel held back. His face was flushed with rage. Without taking his eyes off Gabriel, the *contratista* slid into his truck and sped off, leaving us in a cloud of dust.

I felt scared. I had not seen men fight before. My mouth felt dry and my hands and legs began to shake. Gabriel threw his hat on the ground and said angrily, "That Díaz is a coward. He thinks he's a big man because he runs the *bracero* camp for the growers. He's nothing but a leech! And now he tries to treat me like an animal. I've had it." Then, picking up his hat and putting it on, he added, "He can cheat me out of my money. He can fire me. But he can't force me to do what isn't right. He can't take away my dignity. That he can't do!"

All day, while Gabriel and I hoed weeds, I kept thinking about what happened that morning. It made me angry and sad. Gabriel cursed as he hacked at the weeds.

When I got home from work that evening, I felt restless. I went outside to play kick-the-can. "Come on guys, let's play!" Carlos yelled out, resting his right foot on the can.

I went up to Manuelito who was sitting on the ground and leaning against one of the garbage cans. "You heard Carlos, let's play," I said loudly so that Carlos could hear me.

"He didn't mean me," Manuelito answered, slowly getting up.

"Yes, you too," I insisted.

"Is it true, Carlos?" Manuelito asked.

"No way!" Carlos shouted.

Manuelito put his hands in his pockets and walked away.

"If Manuelito doesn't play, I won't either," I said. As soon as I said it, my heart started pounding. My knees felt weak. Carlos came right up to me. He had fire in his eyes. "Manuelito doesn't play!" he yelled.

He stuck his right foot behind my feet and pushed me. I fell flat on my back. My brothers rushed over to help me up. "You can push me around, but you can't force me to play!" I yelled back, dusting off my clothes and walking away. Trampita, Torito, Rubén, and Manuelito followed me to the front of our barrack.

Carlos stood alone inside the circle in the dirt, looking at the can and glancing at us once in a while. After a few moments, he cocked his head back, spat on the ground, and swaggered toward us saying, "Okay, Manuelito can play."

Screaming with joy, Manuelito and my brothers jumped up and down like grasshoppers. I felt like celebrating, too, but I held back. I did not want Carlos to see how happy I was.

The following morning, when Ito told us that the *contratista* had gotten Gabriel fired and sent back to Mexico, I felt like someone had kicked me in the stomach. I could not concentrate on work. At times I found myself not moving at all. By the time I had picked one crate, Papá had picked two. He finished his row, started a second, and caught up to me.

"What's the matter, Panchito?" he asked. "You're moving too slow. You need to speed it up."

"I keep thinking about Gabriel," I answered.

"What Díaz did was wrong, and someday he'll pay for it, if not in this life, in the next one," he said. "Gabriel did what he had to do."

Papá pushed me along, handing me several handfuls of strawberries he picked from my row. With his help, I got through that long day.

When we got home from work, I did not want to play kick-the-can. I wanted to be alone, but my brothers

95

would not let me. They followed me around, asking me to play.

I finally gave in when Manuelito came over and joined them. "Please, just one game," he pleaded.

"Okay, just one," I answered.

We drew sticks to see who would play guard. Carlos was it. While he counted to twenty with his eyes closed, we ran and hid. I went behind a pepper tree that was next to the outhouse. When Carlos spotted me, he shouted, "I spy Panchito!" We both raced to the can. I got to it first and kicked it with all my might. It went up in the air and landed in one of the garbage cans. That was the last time I played the game.

THE BAT-POET

Randall Jarrell

Once upon a time there was a bat—a little light brown bat, the color of coffee with cream in it. He looked like a furry mouse with wings. When I'd go in and out of my front door, in the daytime, I'd look up over my head and see him hanging upside down from the roof of the porch. He and the others hung there in a bunch, all snuggled together with their wings folded, fast asleep. Sometimes one of them would wake up for a minute and get in a more comfortable position, and then the others would wiggle around in their sleep till they'd get more comfortable too; when they all moved it looked as if a fur wave went over them. At night they'd fly up and down, around and around, and catch insects and eat them; on a rainy night, though, they'd stay snuggled together just as though it were still day. If you pointed a flashlight at them you'd see them screw up their faces to keep the light out of their eyes.

Toward the end of summer, all the bats except the little brown one began sleeping in the barn. He missed them, and tried to get them to come back and sleep on the porch with him. "What do you want to sleep in the barn for?" he asked them.

"We don't know," the others said. "What do you want to sleep on the porch for?"

"It's where we always sleep," he said. "If I slept in the barn I'd be homesick. Do come back and sleep with me!" But they wouldn't.

So he had to sleep all alone. He missed the others. They had always felt so warm and furry against him; whenever he'd waked, he'd pushed himself up into the middle of them and gone right back to sleep. Now he'd wake up and, instead of snuggling against the others and going back to sleep, he would just hang there and think. Sometimes he would open his eyes a little and look out into the sunlight. It gave him a queer feeling for it to be daytime and for him to be hanging there looking; he felt the way you would feel if you woke up and went to the window and stayed there for hours, looking out into the moonlight.

It was different in the daytime. The squirrels and the chipmunk, that he had never seen before—at night they were curled up in their nests or holes, fast asleep—ate nuts and acorns and seeds, and ran after each other playing. And all the birds hopped and sang and flew;

at night they had been asleep, except for the mockingbird. The bat had always heard the mockingbird. The mockingbird would sit on the highest branch of a tree in the moonlight, and sing half the night. The bat loved to listen to him. He could imitate all the other birds—he'd even imitate the way the squirrels chattered when they were angry, like two rocks being knocked together; and he could imitate the milk bottles being put down on the porch and the barn door closing, a long, rusty squeak. And he made up songs and words all his own, that nobody else had ever said or sung.

The bat told the other bats about all the things you could see and hear in the daytime. "You'd love them," he said. "The next time you wake up in the daytime, just keep your eyes open for a while and don't go back to sleep."

The other bats were sure they wouldn't like that. "We wish we didn't wake up at all," they said. "When you wake up in the daytime the light hurts your eyes—the thing to do is to close them and go right back to sleep. Day's to sleep in; as soon as it's night we'll open our eyes."

"But won't you even try it?" the little brown bat said. "Just for once, try it."

The bats all said, "No."

"But why not?" asked the little brown bat.

The bats said, "We don't know. We just don't want to."

"At least listen to the mockingbird. When you hear him it's just like the daytime."

The other bats said, "He sounds so queer. If only he squeaked or twittered—but he keeps shouting in that bass voice of his." They said this because the mockingbird's voice sounded terribly loud and deep to them; they always made little high twittering sounds themselves.

"Once you get used to it you'll like it," the little bat said. "Once you get used to it, it sounds wonderful."

"All right," said the others, "we'll try." But they were just being polite; they didn't try.

The little brown bat kept waking up in the daytime, and kept listening to the mockingbird, until one day he thought, "*I* could make up a song like the mockingbird's." But when he tried, his high notes were all high and his low notes were all high and the notes in between were all high: he couldn't make a tune. So he imitated the mockingbird's words instead. At first his words didn't go together—even the bat could see that they didn't sound a bit like the mockingbird's. But after a while some of them began to sound beautiful, so that the bat said to himself, "If you get the words right you don't need a tune."

The bat went over and over his words till he could say them off by heart. That night he said them to the other bats. "I've made the words like the mockingbird's," he told them, "so you can tell what it's like in the daytime." Then he said to them in a deep voice—he couldn't help imitating the mockingbird—his words about the daytime:

At dawn, the sun shines like a million moons
And all the shadows are as bright as moonlight.
The birds begin to sing with all their might.
The world awakens and forgets the night.

The black-and-gray turns green-and-gold-and-blue.
The squirrels begin to—

But when he'd got this far the other bats just couldn't keep quiet any longer.

"The sun *hurts*," said one. "It hurts like getting something in your eyes."

"That's right," said another. "And shadows are black— how can a shadow be bright?"

Another one said, "What's green-and-gold-and-blue? When you say things like that we don't know what you mean."

"And it's just not real," the first one said. "When the sun rises the world goes to sleep."

"But go on," said one of the others. "We didn't mean to interrupt you."

"No, we're sorry we interrupted you," all the others said. "Say us the rest."

But when the bat tried to say them the rest he couldn't remember a word. It was hard to say anything at all, but finally he said, "I—I—tomorrow I'll say you the rest." Then he flew back to the porch. There were lots of insects flying around the light, but he didn't catch a one; instead he flew to his rafter, hung there upside down with his wings folded, and after a while went to sleep.

But he kept on making poems like the mockingbird's—only now he didn't say them to the bats. One night he saw a mother possum, with all her little white baby possums holding tight to her, eating the fallen apples under the apple tree; one night an owl swooped down on him and came so close he'd have caught him if the bat hadn't flown into a hole in the old oak by the side of the house; and another time four squirrels spent the whole morning chasing each other up and down trees, across the lawn, and over the roof. He made up poems about them all. Sometimes the poem would make him think, "It's like the mockingbird! This time it's really like the mockingbird!" But sometimes the poem would seem so bad to him that he'd get discouraged and stop in the middle, and by the next day he'd have forgotten it.

When he would wake up in the daytime and hang there looking out at the colors of the world, he would say the poems over to himself. He wanted to say them to the other bats, but then he would remember what had happened when he'd said them before. There was nobody for him to say the poems to.

One day he thought, "I could say them to the mockingbird." It got to be a regular thought of his. It was a long time, though, before he really went to the mockingbird.

The mockingbird had bad days when he would try to drive everything out of the yard, no matter what it was. He always had a peremptory, authoritative look, as if he were more alive than anything else and wanted everything else to know it; on his bad days he'd dive on everything that came into the yard—on cats and dogs, even—and strike at them with his little sharp beak and sharp claws. On his good days he didn't pay so much attention to the world, but just sang.

The day the bat went to him the mockingbird was perched on the highest branch of the big willow by the porch, singing with all his might. He was a clear gray, with white bars across his wings that flashed when he flew; every part of him had a clear, quick, decided look about it. He was standing on tiptoe, singing and singing and singing; sometimes he'd spring up into the air. This time he was singing a song about mockingbirds.

The bat fluttered to the nearest branch, hung upside down from it, and listened; finally when the mockingbird stopped just for a moment he said in his little high voice, "It's beautiful, just beautiful!"

"You like poetry?" asked the mockingbird. You could tell from the way he said it that he was surprised.

"I love it," said the bat. "I listen to you every night. Every day too. I—I—"

"It's the last poem I've composed," said the mockingbird. "It's called 'To a Mockingbird.'"

"It's wonderful," the bat said. "Wonderful! Of all the songs I ever heard you sing, it's the best."

This pleased the mockingbird—mockingbirds love to be told that their last song is the best. "I'll sing it for you again," the mockingbird offered.

"Oh, please do sing it again," said the bat. "I'd love to hear it again. Just love to! Only when you've finished could I—"

But the mockingbird had already started. He not only sang it again, he made up new parts, and sang them over and over and over; they were so beautiful that the bat forgot about his own poem and just listened. When the mockingbird had finished, the bat thought, "No, I just can't say him mine. Still, though—" He said to the mockingbird, "It's wonderful to get to hear you. I could listen to you forever."

"It's a pleasure to sing to such a responsive audience," said the mockingbird. "Anytime you'd like to hear it again just tell me."

The bat said, "Could—could—"

"Yes?" said the mockingbird.

The bat went on in a shy voice, "Do you suppose that I—that I could—"

The mockingbird said warmly, "That you could hear it again? Of course you can. I'll be delighted." And he sang it all over again. This time it was the best of all.

The bat told him so, and the mockingbird looked pleased but modest; it was easy for him to look pleased but hard for him to look modest, he was so full of himself. The bat asked him, "Do you suppose a bat could make poems like yours?"

"A *bat*?" the mockingbird said. But then he went on politely, "Well, I don't see why not. He couldn't sing them, of course—he simply doesn't have the range; but that's no reason he couldn't make them up. Why, I suppose for bats a bat's poems would be ideal."

The bat said, "Sometimes when I wake up in the daytime I make up poems. Could I—I wonder whether I could say you one of *my* poems?"

A queer look came over the mockingbird's face, but he said cordially, "I'd be delighted to hear one. Go right ahead." He settled himself on his branch with a listening expression.

The bat said:

> A shadow is floating through the moonlight
> Its wings don't make a sound.
> Its claws are long, its beak is bright.
> Its eyes try all the corners of the night.
>
> It calls and calls: all the air swells and heaves
> And washes up and down like water.
> The ear that listens to the owl believes
> In death. The bat beneath the eaves,
>
> The mouse beside the stone are still as death—
> The owl's air washes them like water.
> The owl goes back and forth inside the night,
> And the night holds its breath.

When he'd finished his poem the bat waited for the mockingbird to say something; he didn't know it, but he was holding his breath.

"Why, I like it," said the mockingbird. "Technically it's quite accomplished. The way you change the rhyme scheme's particularly effective."

The bat said, "It is?"

"Oh yes," said the mockingbird. "And it was clever of you to have that last line two feet short."

The bat said blankly, "Two feet short?"

"It's two feet short," said the mockingbird a little impatiently. "The next-to-the-last line's iambic pentameter, and the last line's iambic trimeter."

The bat looked so bewildered that the mockingbird said in a kind voice, "An iambic foot has one weak syllable and one strong syllable; the weak one comes first. That last line of yours has six syllables and the one before it has ten; when you shorten the last line like that it gets the effect of the night holding its breath."

"I didn't know that," the bat said. "I just made it like holding your breath."

"To be sure, to be sure!" said the mockingbird. "I enjoyed your poem very much. When you've made up some more do come round and say me another."

The bat said that he would, and fluttered home to his rafter. Partly he felt very good—the mockingbird had liked his poem—and partly he felt just terrible. He thought, "Why, I might as well have said it to the bats. What do I care how many feet it has? The owl nearly kills me, and he says he likes the rhyme scheme!" He hung there upside down, thinking bitterly. After a while he said to himself, "The trouble isn't making poems, the trouble's finding somebody that will listen to them."

Before he went to sleep he said his owl poem over to himself, and it seemed to him that it was exactly like the owl. "The *owl* would like it," he thought. "If only I could say it to the owl!"

And then he thought, "That's it! I can't say it to the owl, I don't dare get that near him; but if I made up a poem about the chipmunk I could say it to the chipmunk—*he'd* be interested." The bat got so excited his fur stood up straight and he felt warm all over. He thought, "I'll go to the chipmunk and say, 'If you'll give me six crickets I'll make a poem about you.' Really I'd do it for nothing; but they don't respect something if they get it for nothing. I'll say, 'For six crickets I'll do your portrait in verse.' "

The next day, at twilight, the bat flew to the chipmunk's hole. The chipmunk had dozens of holes, but the bat had noticed that there was one he liked best and always slept in. Before long the chipmunk ran up, his cheeks bulging. "Hello," said the bat.

The instant he heard the bat the chipmunk froze; then he dived into his hole. "Wait! Wait!" the bat cried. But the chipmunk had disappeared. "Come back," the bat called. "I won't hurt you." But he had to talk for a long time before the chipmunk came back, and even then he just stuck the tip of his nose out of the hole.

The bat hardly knew how to begin, but he timidly said to the chipmunk, who listened timidly, "I thought of making this offer to—to the animals of the vicinity. You're the first one I've made it to."

The chipmunk didn't say anything. The bat gulped, and said quickly, "For only six crickets I'll do your portrait in verse."

The chipmunk said, "What are crickets?"

The bat felt discouraged. "I knew I might have to tell him about poems," he thought, "but I never thought I'd have to tell him about *crickets*." He explained, "They're little black things you see on the porch at night, by the light. They're awfully good. But that's all right about them; instead of crickets you could give me—well, this time you don't have to give me anything. It's a—an introductory offer."

The chipmunk said in a friendly voice, "I don't understand."

"I'll make you a poem about yourself," said the bat. "One just about you." He saw from the look in the chipmunk's eyes that the chipmunk didn't understand. The bat said, "I'll say you a poem about the owl, and then you'll see what it's like."

He said his poem and the chipmunk listened intently; when the poem was over the chipmunk gave a big shiver and said, "It's terrible, just terrible! Is there really something like that at night?"

The bat said, "If it weren't for that hole in the oak he'd have got *me*."

The chipmunk said in a determined voice, "I'm going to bed earlier. Sometimes when there're lots of nuts I stay out till it's pretty dark; but believe me, I'm never going to again."

The bat said, "It's a pleasure to say a poem to—to such a responsive audience. Do you want me to start on the poem about you?"

The chipmunk said thoughtfully, "I don't have enough holes. It'd be awfully easy to dig some more holes."

"Shall I start on the poem about you?" asked the bat.

"All right," said the chipmunk. "But could you put in lots of holes? The first thing in the morning I'm going to dig myself another."

"I'll put in a lot," the bat promised. "Is there anything else you'd like to have in it?"

The chipmunk thought for a minute and said, "Well, nuts. And seeds—those big fat seeds they have in the feeder."

"All right," said the bat. "Tomorrow afternoon I'll be back. Or day after tomorrow—I don't really know how long it will take." He and the chipmunk said goodbye to each other and he fluttered home to the porch. As soon as he got comfortably settled he started to work on the poem about the chipmunk. But somehow he kept coming back to the poem about the owl, and what the chipmunk had said, and how he'd looked. "*He* didn't say any of that two-feet-short stuff!" The bat hung there upside down, trying to work on his new poem. He was happy.

When at last he'd finished the poem—it took him longer than he'd thought—he went looking for the chipmunk. It was a bright afternoon, and the sun blazed in the bat's eyes, so that everything looked blurred and golden. When he met the chipmunk hurrying down the path that ran past the old stump, he thought, "What a beautiful color he is! Why, the fur back on his tail's rosy, almost. And those lovely black and white stripes on his back!"

"Hello," he said.

"Hello," said the chipmunk. "Is it done yet?"

"All done," said the bat happily. "I'll say it to you. It's named 'The Chipmunk's Day.'"

The chipmunk said in a pleased voice, "My day." He sat there and listened while the bat said:

> In and out the bushes, up the ivy,
> Into the hole
> By the old oak stump, the chipmunk flashes.
> Up the pole.
>
> To the feeder full of seeds he dashes,
> Stuffs his cheeks.
> The chickadee and titmouse scold him.
> Down he streaks.
>
> Red as the leaves the wind blows off the maple,
> Red as a fox,
> Striped like a skunk, the chipmunk whistles
> Past the love seat, past the mailbox,
>
> Down the path,
> Home to his warm hole stuffed with sweet
> Things to eat.
> Neat and slight and shining, his front feet
>
> Curled at his breast, he sits there while the sun
> Stripes the red west
> With its last light: the chipmunk
> Dives to his rest.

When he'd finished, the bat asked, "Do you like it?"

For a moment the chipmunk didn't say anything, then he said in a surprised, pleased voice, "Say it again." The bat said it again. When he'd finished, the chipmunk said, "Oh, it's *nice*. It all goes in and out, doesn't it?"

The bat was so pleased he didn't know what to say. "Am I really as red as that?" asked the chipmunk.

"Oh yes," the bat said.

"You put in the seeds and the hole and everything," exclaimed the chipmunk. "I didn't think you could. I thought you'd make me more like the owl." Then he said, "Say me the one about the owl."

The bat did. The chipmunk said, "It makes me shiver. Why do I like it if it makes me shiver?"

"I don't know. I see why the owl would like it, but I don't see why we like it."

"Who are you going to do now?" asked the chipmunk.

The bat said, "I don't know. I haven't thought about anybody but you. Maybe I could do a bird."

"Why don't you do the cardinal? He's red and black like me, and he eats seeds at the feeder like me—you'd be in practice."

The bat said doubtfully, "I've watched him, but I don't know him."

"I'll ask him," said the chipmunk. "I'll tell him what it's like, and then he's sure to want to."

"That's awfully nice of you," said the bat. "I'd love to

do one about him. I like to watch him feed his babies."

The next day, while the bat was hanging from his rafter fast asleep, the chipmunk ran up the ivy to the porch and called to the bat, "He wants you to." The bat stirred a little and blinked his eyes, and the chipmunk said, "The cardinal wants you to. I had a hard time telling him what a poem was like, but after I did he wanted you to."

"All right," said the bat sleepily. "I'll start it tonight."

The chipmunk said, "What did you say I was as red as? I don't mean a fox. I remember that."

"As maple leaves. As leaves the wind blows off the maple."

"Oh yes, I remember now," the chipmunk said; he ran off contentedly.

When the bat woke up that night he thought, "Now I'll begin on the cardinal." He thought about how red the cardinal was, and how he sang, and what he ate, and how he fed his big brown babies. But somehow he couldn't get started.

All the next day he watched the cardinal. The bat hung from his rafter, a few feet from the feeder, and whenever the cardinal came to the feeder he'd stare at him and hope he'd get an idea. It was queer the way the cardinal cracked the sunflower seeds; instead of standing on them and hammering them open, like a titmouse, he'd turn them over and over in his beak—it gave him a thoughtful look—and all at once the seed would fall open, split in two. While the cardinal was cracking the seed his two babies stood underneath him on tiptoe, fluttering their wings and quivering all over, their mouths wide open. They were a beautiful soft bright brown—even their beaks were brown—and they were already as big as their father. Really they were old enough to feed themselves, and did whenever he wasn't there; but as long as he was there they begged and begged, till the father would fly down by one and stuff the seed in its mouth, while the other quivered and cheeped as if its heart were breaking. The father was such a beautiful clear bright red, with his tall crest the wind rippled like fur, that it didn't seem right for him to be so harried and useful and hard-working: it was like seeing a general in a red uniform washing hundreds and hundreds of dishes. The babies followed him everywhere, and kept sticking their open mouths up by his mouth—they shook all over, they begged so hard—and he never got a bite for himself.

But it was no use: no matter how much the bat watched, he never got an idea. Finally he went to the chipmunk and said in a perplexed voice, "I can't make up a poem about the cardinal."

The chipmunk said, "Why, just say what he's like, the way you did with the owl and me."

"I would if I could," the bat said, "but I can't. I don't

know why I can't, but I can't. I watch him and he's just beautiful, he'd make a beautiful poem; but I can't think of anything."

"That's *queer*," the chipmunk said.

The bat said in a discouraged voice, "I guess I can't make portraits of the animals after all."

"What a shame!"

"Oh well," the bat said, "it was just so I'd have somebody to say them to. Now that I've got you I'm all right—when I get a good idea I'll make a poem about it and say it to you."

"I'll tell the cardinal you couldn't," the chipmunk said. "He won't be too disappointed, he never has heard a poem. I tried to tell him what they're like, but I don't think he really understood."

He went off to tell the cardinal, and the bat flew home. He felt relieved; it was wonderful not to have to worry about the cardinal anymore.

All morning the mockingbird had been chasing everything out of the yard—he gave you the feeling that having anything else in the world was more than he could bear. Finally he flew up to the porch, sat on the arm of the chair, and began to chirp in a loud, impatient, demanding way, until the lady who lived inside brought him out some raisins. He flew up to a branch, waited impatiently, and as soon as she was gone dived down on the raisins and ate up every one. Then he flew over the willow and began to sing with all his might.

The bat clung to his rafter, listening drowsily. Sometimes he would open his eyes a little, and the sunlight and the shadows and the red and yellow and orange branches waving in the wind made a kind of blurred pattern, so that he would blink, and let his eyelids steal together, and go contentedly back to sleep. When he woke up it was almost dark; the sunlight was gone, and the red and yellow and orange leaves were all gray, but the mockingbird was still singing.

The porch light was lit, and there were already dozens of insects circling round it. As the bat flew toward them he felt hungry but comfortable.

Just then the mockingbird began to imitate a jay—not the way a jay squawks or scolds but the way he really sings, in a deep soft voice; as he listened the bat remembered how the mockingbird had driven off two jays that morning. He thought, "It's queer the way he drives everything off and then imitates it. You wouldn't think that—"

And at that instant he had an idea for a poem. The insects were still flying round and round the light, the mockingbird was still imitating the jay, but the bat didn't eat and he didn't listen; he flapped slowly and thoughtfully back to his rafter and began to work on the poem.

When he finally finished it—he worked on it off and on for two nights—he flew off to find the chipmunk. "I've got a new one," he said happily.

"What's it about?"

"The mockingbird."

"The mockingbird!" the chipmunk repeated. "Say it to me." He was sitting up with his paws on his chest, looking intently at the bat—it was the way he always listened.

The bat said:

Look one way and the sun is going down,
Look the other and the moon is rising.
The sparrow's shadow's longer than the lawn.
The bats squeak, "Night is here," the birds cheep,
    "Day is gone."
On the willow's highest branch, monopolizing
Day and night, cheeping, squeaking, soaring,
The mockingbird is imitating life.

All day the mockingbird has owned the yard.
As light first woke the world, the sparrows trooped
Onto the seedy lawn: the mockingbird
Chased them off shrieking. Hour by hour, fighting hard
To make the world his own, he swooped
On thrushes, thrashers, jays, and chickadees—
At noon he drove away a big black cat.

Now, in the moonlight, he sits here and sings.
A thrush is singing, then a thrasher, then a jay—
Then, all at once, a cat begins meowing.
A mockingbird can sound like anything.
He imitates the world he drove away
So well that for a minute, in the moonlight,
Which one's the mockingbird? Which one's the world?

When he had finished, the chipmunk didn't say anything; the bat said uneasily, "Did you like it?"

For a minute the chipmunk didn't answer him. Then he said, "It really is like him. You know, he's chased me. And can he imitate me! You wouldn't think he'd drive you away and imitate you. You wouldn't think he could."

The bat could see that what the chipmunk said meant that he liked the poem, but he couldn't keep from saying, "You do like it?"

The chipmunk said, "Yes, I like it. But he won't like it."

"You liked the one about you," the bat said.

"Yes," the chipmunk answered. "But he won't like the one about him."

The bat said, "But it is like him."

The chipmunk said, "Just like. Why don't you go say it to him? I'll go with you."

When they found the mockingbird—it was one of his good days—the bat told him that he had made up a new poem. "Could I say it to you?" he asked. He sounded timid—guilty almost.

"To be sure, to be sure!" answered the mockingbird, and put on his listening expression.

The bat said, "It's a poem about—well, about mockingbirds."

The mockingbird repeated, "About mockingbirds!" His face had changed, so that he had to look listening all over again. Then the bat repeated to the mockingbird his poem about the mockingbird. The mockingbird listened intently, staring at the bat; the chipmunk listened intently, staring at the mockingbird.

When the bat had finished, nobody said anything. Finally the chipmunk said, "Did it take you long to make it up?"

Before the bat could answer, the mockingbird exclaimed angrily, "You sound as if there were something wrong with imitating things!"

"Oh no," the bat said.

"Well then, you sound as if there were something wrong with driving them off. It's my territory, isn't it? If you can't drive things off your own territory what can you do?"

The bat didn't know what to say; after a minute the chipmunk said uneasily, "He just meant it's odd to drive them all off and then imitate them so well too."

"Odd!" cried the mockingbird. "Odd! If I didn't it really would be odd. Did you ever hear of a mockingbird that didn't?"

The bat said politely, "No indeed. No, it's just what mockingbirds do do. That's really why I made up the poem about it—I admire mockingbirds so much, you know."

The chipmunk said, "He talks about them all the time."

"A mockingbird's sensitive," said the mockingbird; when he said sensitive his voice went way up and way back down. "They get on my nerves. You just don't understand how much they get on my nerves. Sometimes I think if I can't get rid of them I'll go crazy."

"If they didn't get on your nerves so, maybe you wouldn't be able to imitate them so well," the chipmunk said in a helpful, hopeful voice.

"And the way they sing!" cried the mockingbird. "One two three, one two three—the same thing, the same thing, always the same old thing! If only they'd just once sing something different!"

The bat said, "Yes, I can see how hard on you it must be. I meant for the poem to show that, but I'm afraid I must not have done it right."

"You just haven't any idea!" the mockingbird went on, his eyes flashing and his feathers standing up. "Nobody but a mockingbird has any idea!"

The bat and the chipmunk were looking at the mockingbird with the same impressed, uneasy look. From then on they were very careful what they said— mostly they just listened, while the mockingbird told them what it was like to be a mockingbird. Toward the end he seemed considerably calmer and more cheerful, and even told the bat he had enjoyed hearing his poem.

The bat looked pleased, and asked the mockingbird, "Did you like the way I rhymed the first lines of the stanzas and then didn't rhyme the last two?"

The mockingbird said shortly, "I didn't notice"; the chipmunk told the mockingbird how much he always enjoyed hearing the mockingbird sing; and, a little later, the bat and the chipmunk told the mockingbird goodbye.

When they had left, the two of them looked at each other and the bat said, "You were right."

"Yes," said the chipmunk. Then he said, "I'm glad I'm not a mockingbird."

"I'd like to be because of the poems," the bat said, "but as long as I'm not, I'm glad I'm not."

"He thinks that he's different from everything else," the chipmunk said, "and he is."

The bat said, just as if he hadn't heard the chipmunk, "I wish I could make up a poem about bats."

The chipmunk asked, "Why don't you?"

"If I had one about bats, maybe I could say it to the bats."

"That's right."

For weeks he wished that he had the poem. He would hunt all night, and catch and eat hundreds and hundreds of gnats and moths and crickets, and all the time he would be thinking, "If only I could make up a poem about bats!" One day he dreamed that it was done and that he was saying it to them, but when he woke up all he could remember was the way it ended:

> At sunrise, suddenly the porch was bats:
> A thousand bats were hanging from the rafter.

It had sounded wonderful in his dream, but now it just made him wish that the bats still slept on the porch.

He felt cold and lonely. Two squirrels had climbed up in the feeder and were making the same queer noise—a kind of whistling growl—to scare each other away; somewhere on the other side of the house the mockingbird was singing. The bat shut his eyes.

For some reason, he began to think of the first things he could remember. Till a bat is two weeks old he's never alone: the little naked thing—he hasn't even any fur—clings to his mother wherever she goes. After that she leaves him at night; and the other babies hang there sleeping, till at last their mothers come home to them. Sleepily, almost dreaming, the bat began to make up a poem about a mother and her baby.

It was easier than the other poems, somehow: all he had to do was remember what it had been like and every once in a while put in a rhyme. But easy as it was, he kept getting tired and going to sleep, and would forget parts and have to make them over. When at last he finished he went to say it to the chipmunk.

The trees were all bare, and the wind blew the leaves past the chipmunk's hole; it was cold. When the chipmunk stuck his head out it looked fatter than the bat had ever seen it. The chipmunk said in a slow, dazed voice, "It's all full. My hole's all full." Then he exclaimed surprisedly to the bat, "How fat you are!"

"I?" the bat asked. "I'm fat?" Then he realized it was so; for weeks he had been eating and eating and eating. He said, "I've done my poem about the bats. It's about a mother and her baby."

"Say it to me."
The bat said:

A bat is born
Naked and blind and pale.
His mother makes a pocket of her tail
And catches him. He clings to her long fur
By his thumbs and toes and teeth.
And then the mother dances through the night
Doubling and looping, soaring, somersaulting—
Her baby hangs on underneath.
All night, in happiness, she hunts and flies.
Her high sharp cries
Like shining needlepoints of sound
Go out into the night and, echoing back,
Tell her what they have touched.
She hears how far it is, how big it is,
Which way it's going:
She lives by hearing.
The mother eats the moths and gnats she catches
In full flight; in full flight
The mother drinks the water of the pond
She skims across. Her baby hangs on tight.
Her baby drinks the milk she makes him
In moonlight or starlight, in mid-air.
Their single shadow, printed on the moon
Or fluttering across the stars,
Whirls on all night; at daybreak
The tired mother flaps home to her rafter.
The others all are there.
They hang themselves up by their toes,
They wrap themselves in their brown wings.

Bunches upside down, they sleep in air.
Their sharp ears, their sharp teeth, their quick
   sharp faces
Are dull and slow and mild.
All the bright day, as the mother sleeps,
She folds her wings about her sleeping child.

When the bat had finished, the chipmunk said, "It's all really so?"

"Why, of course," the bat said.

"And you do all that too? If you shut your eyes and make a noise you can hear where I am and which way I'm going?"

"Of course."

The chipmunk shook his head and said wonderingly, "You bats sleep all day and fly all night, and see with your ears, and sleep upside down, and eat while you're flying and drink while you're flying, and turn somersaults in mid-air with your baby hanging on, and—and—it's really queer."

The bat said, "Did you like the poem?"

"Oh, of course. Except I forgot it was a poem. I just kept thinking how queer it must be to be a bat."

The bat said, "No, it's not queer. It's wonderful to fly all night. And when you sleep all day with the others it feels wonderful."

The chipmunk yawned. "The end of it made me all sleepy," he said. "But I was already sleepy. I'm sleepy all the time now."

The bat thought, "Why, I am too." He said to the chipmunk, "Yes, it's winter. It's almost winter."

"You ought to say the poem to the other bats," the chipmunk said. "They'll like it just the way I liked the one about me."

"Really?"

"I'm sure of it. When it has all the things you do, you can't help liking it."

"Thank you so much for letting me say it to you," the bat said. "I will say it to them. I'll go say it to them now."

"Goodbye," said the chipmunk. "I'll see you soon. Just as soon as I wake up I'll see you."

"Goodbye," the bat said.

The chipmunk went back into his hole. It was strange to have him move so heavily, and to see his quick face so slow. The bat flew slowly off to the barn. In the west, over the gray hills, the sun was red: in a little while the bats would wake up and he could say them the poem.

High up under the roof, in the farthest corner of the barn, the bats were hanging upside down, wrapped in their brown wings. Except for one, they were fast asleep. The one the little brown bat lighted by was asleep; when he felt someone light by him he yawned, and screwed his face up, and snuggled closer to the others. "As soon as he wakes up I'll say it to him," the bat thought. "No, I'll wait till they're all awake." On the other side of him was the bat who was awake: that one gave a

big yawn, snuggled closer to the others, and went back
to sleep.

The bat said to himself sleepily, "I wish I'd said we
sleep all winter. That would have been a good thing to
have in." He yawned. He thought, "It's almost dark. As
soon as it's dark they'll wake up and I'll say them the
poem. The chipmunk said they'd love it." He began to
say the poem over to himself; he said in a soft contented
whisper:

> A bat is born
> Naked and blind and pale.
> His mother makes a pocket of her tail
> And catches him. He clings—he clings—

He tried to think of what came next, but he couldn't
remember. It was about fur, but he couldn't remember
the words that went with it. He went back to the
beginning. He said:

> A bat is born
> Naked and blind—

but before he could get any further he thought, "I wish
I'd said we sleep all winter." His eyes were closed; he
yawned, and screwed his face up, and snuggled closer to
the others.

ACKNOWLEDGMENTS

All possible care has been taken to trace ownership and secure permission for each selection in this series. The Great Books Foundation wishes to thank the following authors, publishers, and representatives for permission to reprint copyrighted material:

The No-Guitar Blues, from BASEBALL IN APRIL AND OTHER STORIES, by Gary Soto. Copyright © 1990 by Gary Soto. Reprinted by permission of Harcourt, Inc.

Kaddo's Wall, from THE COW-TAIL SWITCH AND OTHER WEST AFRICAN STORIES, by Harold Courlander and George Herzog. Copyright © 1947, 1975 by Harold Courlander. Reprinted by permission of Henry Holt and Company, LLC.

Turquoise Horse, from TURTLE DREAM: COLLECTED STORIES FROM THE HOPI, NAVAHO, PUEBLO, AND HAVASUPAI, by Gerald Hausman. Copyright © 1989 by Gerald Hausman. Reprinted by permission of Mariposa Publishing and the author.

A Game of Catch, by Richard Wilbur. Copyright © 1953, 1981 by Richard Wilbur. Originally appeared in the *New Yorker*. Reprinted by permission of Harcourt, Inc.

Oliver Hyde's Dishcloth Concert, from RICHARD KENNEDY: COLLECTED STORIES. Copyright © 1977 by Richard Kennedy. Reprinted by permission of the author.

The Hundred-Dollar Bill, by Rose Wilder Lane, from ON THE WAY HOME, by Laura Ingalls Wilder. Copyright © 1962, 1990 by the Little House Heritage Trust. Reprinted by permission of HarperCollins Publishers.

The Invisible Child, from TALES FROM MOOMINVALLEY, by Tove Jansson. Copyright © 1962 by Tove Jansson. Reprinted by permission of Moomin Characters.

IN THE TIME OF THE DRUMS, by Kim L. Siegelson. Copyright © 1999 by Kim L. Siegelson. Reprinted by permission of Hyperion Books for Children.

Learning the Game, from THE CIRCUIT: STORIES FROM THE LIFE OF A MIGRANT CHILD, by Francisco Jiménez. Copyright © 1997 by Francisco Jiménez. Reprinted by permission of the University of New Mexico Press.

THE BAT-POET, by Randall Jarrell. Copyright © 1963, 1964 by Macmillan Publishing Company. Reprinted by permission of Mrs. Randall Jarrell.

ILLUSTRATION CREDITS

Tove Jansson's illustrations for *The Invisible Child* are from TALES FROM MOOMINVALLEY. Illustrations copyright © 1962 by Tove Jannson. Reprinted by permission of Moomin Characters.

Cover art by Terea Shaffer. Copyright © 2006 by Terea Shaffer.

Text and cover design by William Seabright & Associates.

Interior design by Think Design Group.